The War on Terror

POINT
COUNTERPOINT

POINT /////
\\\\\\\\\COUNTERPOINT

The War
on Terror

Paul Ruschmann, J.D.

SERIES CONSULTING EDITOR
Alan Marzilli, M.A., J.D.

CHELSEA HOUSE
P U B L I S H E R S
A Haights Cross Communications Company

Philadelphia

CHELSEA HOUSE PUBLISHERS

VP, New Product Development Sally Cheney
Director of Production Kim Shinners
Creative Manager Takeshi Takahashi
Manufacturing Manager Diann Grasse

Staff for THE WAR ON TERROR

Executive Editor Lee Marcott
Assistant Editor Alexis Browsh
Editorial Assistant Carla Greenberg
Photo Editor Sarah Bloom
Production Editor Noelle Nardone
Series and Cover Designer Keith Trego
Layout 21st Century Publishing and Communications, Inc.

Library of Congress Cataloging-in-Publication Data

Ruschmann, Paul.
  War on terror / Paul Ruschmann.
    p. cm.—(Point/counterpoint series)
Includes bibliographical references and index.
  ISBN 0-7910-8091-9
  1. September 11 Terrorist Attacks, 2001–   2. War on Terrorism, 2001–   —Law and
legislation—United States. 3. Terrorism—United States—Prevention. 4. September 11
Terrorist Attacks, 2001. I. Title. II. Point-counterpoint (Philadelphia, Pa.)
KF9430.R87 2004
363.32'0973—dc22

                                                                    2004017127

CONTENTS

Foreword

Alan Marzilli, M.A., J.D.
Durham, North Carolina

The debates presented in POINT/COUNTERPOINT are among the most interesting and controversial in contemporary American society, but studying them is more than an academic activity. They affect every citizen; they are the issues that today's leaders debate and tomorrow's will decide. The reader may one day play a central role in resolving them.

Why study both sides of the debate? It's possible that the reader will not yet have formed any opinion at all on the subject of this volume—but this is unlikely. It is more likely that the reader will already hold an opinion, probably a strong one, and very probably one formed without full exposure to the arguments of the other side. It is rare to hear an argument presented in a balanced way, and it is easy to form an opinion on too little information; these books will help to fill in the informational gaps that can never be avoided. More important, though, is the practical function of the series: Skillful argumentation requires a thorough knowledge of *both* sides—though there are seldom only two, and only by knowing what an opponent is likely to assert can one form an articulate response.

Perhaps more important is that listening to the other side sometimes helps one to see an opponent's arguments in a more human way. For example, Sister Helen Prejean, one of the nation's most visible opponents of capital punishment, has been deeply affected by her interactions with the families of murder victims. Seeing the families' grief and pain, she understands much better why people support the death penalty, and she is able to carry out her advocacy with a greater sensitivity to the needs and beliefs of those who do not agree with her. Her relativism, in turn, lends credibility to her work. Dismissing the other side of the argument as totally without merit can be too easy—it is far more useful to understand the nature of the controversy and the reasons *why* the issue defies resolution.

The most controversial issues of all are often those that center on a constitutional right. The Bill of Rights—the first ten amendments to the U.S. Constitution—spells out some of the most fundamental rights that distinguish the governmental system of the United States from those that allow fewer (or other) freedoms. But the sparsely worded document is open to interpretation, and clauses of only a few words are often at the heart of national debates. The Bill of Rights was meant to protect individual liberties; but the needs of some individuals clash with those of society as a whole, and when this happens someone has to decide where to draw the line. Thus the Constitution becomes a battleground between the rights of individuals to do as they please and the responsibility of the government to protect its citizens. The First Amendment's guarantee of "freedom of speech," for example, leads to a number of difficult questions. Some forms of expression, such as burning an American flag, lead to public outrage—but nevertheless are said to be protected by the First Amendment. Other types of expression that most people find objectionable, such as sexually explicit material involving children, are not protected because they are considered harmful. The question is not only where to draw the line, but how to do this without infringing on the personal liberties on which the United States was built.

The Bill of Rights raises many other questions about individual rights and the societal "good." Is a prayer before a high school football game an "establishment of religion" prohibited by the First Amendment? Does the Second Amendment's promise of "the right to bear arms" include concealed handguns? Is stopping and frisking someone standing on a corner known to be frequented by drug dealers a form of "unreasonable search and seizure" in violation of the Fourth Amendment? Although the nine-member U.S. Supreme Court has the ultimate authority in interpreting the Constitution, its answers do not always satisfy the public. When a group of nine people—sometimes by a five-to-four vote—makes a decision that affects the lives of hundreds of millions, public outcry can be expected. And the composition of the Court does change over time, so even a landmark decision is not guaranteed to stand forever. The limits of constitutional protection are always in flux.

These issues make headlines, divide courts, and decide elections. They are the questions most worthy of national debate, and this series aims to cover them as thoroughly as possible. Each volume sets out some of the key arguments surrounding a particular issue, even some views that most people consider extreme or radical—but presents a balanced perspective on the issue. Excerpts from the relevant laws and judicial opinions and references to central concepts, source material, and advocacy groups help the reader to explore the issues even further and to read "the letter of the law" just as the legislatures and the courts have established it.

It may seem that some debates—such as those over capital punishment and abortion, debates with a strong moral component—will never be resolved. But American history offers numerous examples of controversies that once seemed insurmountable but now are effectively settled, even if only on the surface. Abolitionists met with widespread resistance to their efforts to end slavery, and the controversy over that issue threatened to cleave the nation in two; but today public debate over the merits of slavery would be unthinkable, though racial inequalities still plague the nation. Similarly unthinkable at one time was suffrage for women and minorities, but this is now a matter of course. Distributing information about contraception once was a crime. Societies change, and attitudes change, and new questions of social justice are raised constantly while the old ones fade into irrelevancy.

Whatever the root of the controversy, the books in POINT/ COUNTERPOINT seek to explain to the reader the origins of the debate, the current state of the law, and the arguments on both sides. The goal of the series is to inform the reader about the issues facing not only American politicians, but all of the nation's citizens, and to encourage the reader to become more actively involved in resolving these debates, as a voter, a concerned citizen, a journalist, an activist, or an elected official. Democracy is based on education, and every voice counts—so every opinion must be an informed one.

———————●——————————●——————————●———————

This volume examines the controversy surrounding the U.S. government's approach to combating international terrorism. The Bush administration treated the 9/11 terrorist attacks as an act of war, even though no foreign government could be directly linked to the attacks. It took an aggressive approach, invading Afghanistan and Iraq, and holding both U.S. and foreign citizens as "enemy combatants" without the same protections afforded to criminal defendants in U.S. courts. Many have questioned both the moral and strategic justification for these military actions in the absence of a declared war and worry that people accused of terrorism have no way to defend themselves against the charges. More ominously, critics of the administration worry that laws such as the Patriot Act, which greatly expanded federal investigators' ability to gather domestic intelligence, threaten the freedom of innocent citizens. However, defenders of anti-terrorism measures insist that strong steps are needed to protect the United States from a new type of war, in which the enemy infiltrates American society, poised to unleash a deadly attack without warning.

September 11, Terrorism, and War

On September 10, 2001, Americans' greatest concern was the economy: rising unemployment, a slumping stock market, and growing fears of a recession. The possibility of a massive terrorist attack was far from their minds: "[M]ost Americans, if asked, would have likely said that their nation had never been more secure. More than a decade after the end of the Cold War, it had become a truism that the world had not seen such a dominant power since ancient Rome."[1]

The Threat of Terrorism

National-security experts, however, were concerned that terrorists were about to attack Americans on their own soil. In 2000, the United States Commission on National Security warned, "Americans are less secure than they believe themselves to be. The time for re-examination is now, before the

American people find themselves shocked by events they never anticipated."[2]

- **Will there be another terrorist attack on America?**

A new and more dangerous terrorist threat first appeared in 1993, when a powerful truck bomb exploded underneath the World Trade Center. After the Trade Center bombing, there were increasingly deadly attacks against Americans overseas, as well as terrorist conspiracies to kill Americans at home.

Authorities linked many of the worst incidents to a worldwide organization known as al Qaeda, which means "the base." Al Qaeda is led by Osama bin Laden, a wealthy Saudi businessman who had embraced a fundamentalist strain of the Islamic faith. Expelled from Saudi Arabia and the Sudan, bin Laden and his followers moved to Afghanistan, where they operated terrorist training camps under the protection of that country's ruling Taliban regime. Bin Laden made no secret of his intentions. In February 1998, he issued a *fatwa*, or religious edict, commanding Muslims to kill Americans, including civilians, anywhere possible. On September 11, 2001, his followers made good on that threat. Terrorists flew passenger jets into the World Trade Center and the Pentagon, killing nearly 3,000 people. Hundreds of thousands witnessed the attacks in person, and billions more around the world saw them on television.

- **Is there a "clash of civilizations" between the West and the Islamic world?**

Responding to September 11

The nation reacted to the attacks with a mixture of grief and outrage. The Bush administration called them an "act of war" and moved quickly to find and punish the terrorists. On September 18, Congress passed a resolution authorizing the president to use "all necessary and appropriate force" against those responsible.

(continued on page 15)

Some Recent Terror Events

- **May 1978:** A package bomb sent to Northwestern University injures a campus police officer. It was the first attack by "Unabomber" Theodore Kaczynski, a violent opponent of technology. Over the next 16 years, his homemade bombs will kill 3 and injure at least 26 others. Kaczynski is arrested in 1996 and later sentenced to life in prison.

- **April 18, 1983:** A Muslim extremist drives a truck filled with explosives into the U.S. embassy in Beirut, Lebanon, killing 63 people, including 17 Americans. The Reagan administration blames Hezbollah, a Muslim guerrilla group, for the bombing and alleges that Iran and Syria provided support to the bombers. Suicide bombing is a new, and deadly, form of terrorism.

- **October 23, 1983:** A truck bomb explodes outside a U.S. Marine barracks in Beirut, killing 241 people. Soon afterward, the United States ends its peacekeeping operations in Lebanon. In May 2003, a federal judge finds that Hezbollah was responsible for the bombing and that high officials in Iran's government approved and funded it.

- **August–September 1984:** In a local election campaign, members of the Rajneesh cult in Oregon contaminate local restaurants with salmonella bacteria in order to make their opponents too sick to vote. About 750 people become seriously ill. It is the nation's worst incidence of food terrorism.

- **April 5, 1986:** A terrorist bomb kills 3 and injures 229, many of them American service personnel, at a Berlin disco. President Reagan blames Libyan leader Muammar Gadafi for the bombing and, on April 15, orders an air strike on alleged terrorist facilities in Libya.

- **December 21, 1988:** A bomb placed on Pan Am Flight 103 explodes over Lockerbie, Scotland, killing 259 people aboard the plane and 11 on the ground. Evidence found at the crash scene links Libyan intelligence agents to the bombing. Libya eventually turns over the suspected terrorists, who are tried under Scottish law, and later agrees to pay $2.7 billion to the victims' families in exchange for an end to American and United Nations economic sanctions.

- **February 26, 1993:** Islamic fundamentalists detonate a bomb underneath the World Trade Center. Four men are tried and found guilty of the bombing in 1994. The alleged mastermind, Ramzi Yousef, is later tried and convicted for planning the bombing, as is Omar Abdel Rahman.

- **April 14, 1993:** Kuwait's security service uncovers a plot by Iraqi agents to kill former President George H. W. Bush with a truck bomb. On June 27, the United States retaliates by launching a cruise missile attack on Iraqi Intelligence Service headquarters in Baghdad.

- **March 20, 1995:** Aum Shinrikyo, a doomsday religious cult, releases nerve gas in six Tokyo subway stations, killing 12 people and sending about 5,000 to hospitals. It is the first large-scale terrorist attack using chemical weapons.

- **April 19, 1995**: A truck bomb explodes outside the Alfred P. Murrah Federal Building in Oklahoma City, killing 168 people. Timothy McVeigh and Terry Nichols, army veterans with ties to extreme right-wing causes, are charged. McVeigh is sentenced to death, Nichols to life in prison. Many believe that the two men did not act alone and that international terrorists were involved. The bombing prompts Congress to pass a new antiterrorism law in 1996.

- **June 25, 1996:** A truck bomb explodes outside American military apartments in al-Khobar, Saudi Arabia, killing 19 and injuring hundreds. Federal prosecutors later allege that Hezbollah terrorists were responsible and that Iranian officials lent them support.

- **July 27, 1996:** A pipe bomb planted at the Olympic Games in Atlanta kills 1 person and injures 111. In November 2000, federal authorities charge Eric Robert Rudolph, a Christian extremist, for that bombing. He is finally apprehended in June 2003. Rudolph also has been charged in connection with the bombing of three abortion clinics and a gay nightclub.

- **August 7, 1998:** Simultaneous truck bombs explode outside the American embassies in Kenya and Tanzania, killing 225 and injuring more than 4,000. On August 20, the United States retaliates by launching cruise missile attacks on a suspected nerve gas factory in the Sudan and terrorist training camps in Afghanistan. Federal prosecutors accuse Osama bin Laden of orchestrating the bombings and file charges against a number of his followers. In May 2001, four men are convicted for their role in the bombings. Their trial reveals details about al Qaeda's organization and business dealings.

- **October 12, 2000:** A bomb explodes near the destroyer U.S.S. Cole at Aden, Yemen, killing 17, injuring 39, and severely damaging the Cole. It is the first time a bomb carried on board a boat is used in a terrorist attack. Federal prosecutors name bin Laden as an unindicted coconspirator.

- **September 11, 2001:** Hijackers fly passenger jets into the World Trade Center and the Pentagon, killing nearly 3,000 people. On October 7, the United States leads an invasion that overthrows Afghanistan's ruling Taliban regime; kills or captures thousands of enemy fighters, including many of al Qaeda's leaders; and dismantles al Qaeda's training camps. In this country, federal authorities arrest more than 1,000 people suspected of having ties to terrorist organizations.

- **October 12, 2002:** Truck bombs destroy two nightclubs in Bali, Indonesia, killing 202 and injuring 200. It is the worst post–September 11 terrorist attack to date. The main suspects are members of Jemaah Islamiyah, an Islamic extremist group with ties to al Qaeda.

- **November 2003:** Suicide bombers attack two synagogues, the British consulate, and a London-based bank in Istanbul, Turkey, killing more than 50 and injuring hundreds. Experts blame the bombings on terrorists who trained in al Qaeda camps but are not under that organization's direct control.

- **March 11, 2004:** A series of bombs at a train station in Madrid, Spain, kills 191 people and injures more than 1,400. Authorities determine that the attacks were carried out by Islamic extremists who were locally organized but that the terrorists had connections to outside fundamentalist groups and might have been overseen by a "supreme leader."

(continued from page 11)

On September 20, the president told a joint session of Congress and the American people that the nation was at war with terrorists. He warned the rest of the world, "Either you are with us, or you are with the terrorists. From this day forward, any nation that continues to harbor or support terrorism will be regarded by the United States as a hostile regime."[3]

He specifically demanded that the Taliban hand over al Qaeda's leaders and close down the terrorist training camps. When the Taliban refused, an American-led military force working with anti-Taliban Afghans known as the Northern Alliance launched an invasion that drove the Taliban out of the country's major cities. Coalition forces killed or captured thousands of Taliban fighters, as well as many of al Qaeda's leaders. Bin Laden himself was not found and is believed to have survived the attack.

> • **If the United States dismantles al Qaeda, will the war on terror be over? Or will other terrorists take their place?**

"A Different Kind of War"

President Bush told the country the fight against terrorism would be a "different kind of war":

> This war will not be like the war against Iraq a decade ago, with a decisive liberation of territory and a swift conclusion. It will not look like the air war above Kosovo two years ago, where no ground troops were used and not a single American was lost in combat. . .
>
> Americans should not expect one battle, but a lengthy campaign, unlike any other we have ever seen. It may include dramatic strikes, visible on TV, and covert operations, secret even in success.[4]

The September 11 attacks have been compared to the bombing of Pearl Harbor, the event that brought the United States into World War II. The September 11 hijackers were a different enemy than the Japanese pilots who bombed Pearl Harbor, however; they lived among Americans while plotting to kill them, were not wearing military uniforms on the day of the attacks, and were not fighting on behalf of a particular country.

> • **What motivates people to kill innocent civilians? Is it ever permissible to do so?**

The invasion of Afghanistan illustrated the difference between traditional conflicts and the war against terror. The target was the Taliban, which few countries recognized as the legitimate government; the Afghan people were, for the most part, innocent bystanders; and it was hard for anti-Taliban fighters to distinguish friends from enemies.

Balancing Liberty and Security

After September 11, the nation's leaders concluded that national security deserved a higher priority, even at the expense of individual liberty. President Bush assumed many of the broad powers of earlier wartime presidents. One of his first actions was to authorize military trials of non-U.S. citizens suspected of involvement in the attacks or membership in terrorist organizations. Meanwhile, federal agents scoured the country looking for people with possible links to terrorists. They asked thousands of men from Arab and Muslim countries why they were in the United States and what they knew about terrorist activity. They also strictly enforced immigration laws and seized the assets of charities and other organizations with suspected ties to terrorist groups.

> • **Is "racial profiling" ever acceptable? Is it an excuse to discriminate against members of minority groups?**

The Bush administration also asked for new legal tools to fight terrorism. Congress quickly responded by passing the USA Patriot Act, a sweeping law that created new terror-related crimes, gave intelligence agencies and the police broader powers to monitor suspected terrorist activity, and made it easier for government agencies to share information.

> • **Are the police using terrorism as an excuse for more power? Will they someday use that power to arrest critics of the government?**

Redefining Foreign Policy

After the September 11 attacks, President Bush announced that the United States would adopt a national-security strategy that focused on preventing future acts of terrorism. In his 2002 State of the Union address, he defined the new threat the nation faced. He singled out Iran, Iraq, and North Korea as an "axis of evil." Those countries were the most dangerous because they had both the motive and the means to provide terrorists with weapons of mass destruction—chemical, biological, or nuclear devices capable of killing thousands, even millions. Given such a threat, the president concluded that a national-security policy developed during the cold war was no longer appropriate: "Deterrence—the promise of massive retaliation against nations—means nothing against shadowy terrorist networks with no nation or citizens to defend. Containment is not possible when unbalanced dictators with weapons of mass destruction can deliver those weapons on missiles or secretly provide them to terrorist allies."[5]

> • **What should the government do to prevent another September 11–type attack? What can citizens do?**

He also made it clear that the United States would not ask other countries' permission before taking action: "While the United States will constantly strive to enlist the support of the international community, we will not hesitate to act alone, if necessary, to exercise our right of self-defense by acting preemptively against such terrorists, to prevent them from doing harm against our people and our country."[6]

The Bush Doctrine was applied first against Iraq. For months, President Bush warned the rest of the world that Iraqi leader Saddam Hussein had weapons of mass destruction. When the United Nations refused to take swift action to disarm Saddam, the president formed a "coalition of the willing" that forcibly removed him from power.

- **Has the United Nations outlived its usefulness? Is the United States trying to sabotage it?**

What Is Terrorism?

Terrorism is as old as history itself, and it has often been associated with religious conflict. Three words in our language—"thug," "zealot," and "assassin"—originally referred to members of ancient Hindu, Jewish, and Muslim extremist sects. Terrorism has been more common during some periods of history than others, and the tactics used by terrorists have changed over the years.

The word "terror" was coined during the French Revolution, when the governing regime used its emergency powers to arrest and execute thousands of accused traitors. France's Reign of Terror was an example of *state terrorism*—violence committed by a government against its own citizens. State terrorism was prevalent in much of the world during the mid-twentieth century. Regimes of both the Left (Mao Zedong's China and Joseph Stalin's Soviet Union) and the Right (Adolf Hitler's Nazi Germany) subjected their enemies to arbitrary arrests, torture, mass imprisonment, and even wholesale slaughter. Nowadays, we associate terrorism with violence committed by individuals, directed at public officials and civilians, and aimed at forcing the government to change its policies.

Many historians trace modern-day terrorism to the radical anarchists of the nineteenth century. Anarchism, a movement against established authority, began in tsarist Russia. Violent anarchists tried to assassinate high government officials in an effort to publicize for their cause. Some also hoped that their actions would provoke a government crackdown that might cause a revolution. The movement spread to other countries, including the United States: In 1901, an anarchist by the name of Leon Czolgosz assassinated President William McKinley.

> • **Are prolife extremists who gun down doctors terrorists? Are environmental activists who destroy property terrorists?**

During the twentieth century, terrorism became part of some countries' struggles for independence; one example is the Republic of Ireland. During World War II, some resistance fighters resorted to terrorism against Nazi occupiers. Terrorism made a comeback during the 1960s, when left-wing guerrillas fought pro-American regimes in Latin America; it spread from there to other parts of the world. Some terrorist movements were *state-supported*: The Soviet Union and Iran lent support to Middle Eastern terrorist groups fighting Israel.

> • **Is terrorism acceptable in a fight for independence? In a revolution against a dictatorship?**

The current wave of terrorism began in the 1980s. It tends to be motivated by religious or ethnic hatred, often uses suicide bombers, and, as September 11 demonstrated, can kill large numbers of civilians. Most of us associate terrorism with the Middle East, but terrorist movements operate in other parts of the world. Non–Middle Eastern terrorist groups include the Shining Path in Peru and the Liberation Tigers of Tamil in Sri Lanka. In this country, there are home-grown terrorists, as well as cells linked to movements based overseas. The most notorious domestic terrorists are right-wing extremists Timothy McVeigh and Terry Nichols, who were responsible for the Oklahoma City bombing.

The war on terror is less black and white than conflicts like World War II are. It is often said that "one man's terrorist is another man's freedom fighter." Many believe that the people of Chechnya, a region in southern Russia, are legitimately fighting for independence. The Russian government treats them as terrorists. The same is true of Palestinians rebelling against Israeli rule in the West Bank and Gaza. There is also a problem of defining what terrorism is. Modern terrorist networks raise money in a number of ways, including asking for donations to fake charities and engaging in crimes such as cigarette smuggling. As a result, it can be difficult to draw

The 1993 World Trade Center Bombing

Shortly after noon on February 26, 1993, more than 1,000 pounds of explosives were detonated in the parking structure under the north tower of the World Trade Center. The explosion killed 6, injured more than 1,000, and caused $300 million in damage.

Investigators concluded that the explosives were loaded onto a van rented by Mohammed Salameh. They tracked down Salameh and soon found other members of the conspiracy: Nidel Ayyad, Ahmad Ajaj, Mahmud Abouhalima, and the alleged mastermind, Ramzi Ahmed Yousef, who fled to Pakistan immediately after the bombing. The men were already under surveillance as potential terrorists. Abouhalima, Ajaj, Ayyad, and Salameh were tried in federal court in New York City.

After the Trade Center bombing, Yousef continued to plan terrorist acts against Americans. In early 1995, he and his followers conspired to bomb 12 commercial airliners in a single day. While making bombs in an apartment in Manila, the Philippines, Yousef started a fire that forced him to flee, leaving behind a computer containing information that led to his arrest in Pakistan. He was brought back to the United States, tried and convicted for plotting the airline bombings, and sentenced to life in prison. Later, in another trial, he was convicted of masterminding the Trade Center bombing.

Authorities came to the conclusion that the Trade Center bombing was part of a wider anti-American campaign by Muslim extremists associated with Osama bin Laden and his al Qaeda organization. Yousef allegedly trained in Afghan terrorist camps and was later linked to al Qaeda. The four convicted bombers were followers of Sheikh Omar Abdel Rahman, an Egyptian cleric whose terrorist organization, Jamaat al-Islamiyya, was connected with al Qaeda. During the 1980s, Rahman worked with Afghan rebels who were fighting the Soviet Union. Because Rahman opposed the Soviets, American authorities allowed him into the country to raise funds for the rebels.

a legal distinction between ordinary crime and lending support to terrorists.

Under the law of armed conflict, the only people allowed to kill others are 'lawful combatants,' those who wear uniforms and carry thier weapons openly. Many terrorist acts are serious violations of the *law of armed conflict*. For centuries, international law has recognized a set of rules governing war. The intent of these

Rahman proved to be no friend of America. After the Soviets left Afghanistan, he turned his anger toward Israel and the United States, urging his followers here to carry out terrorist acts. One of those acts was the assassination of Rabbi Meir Kahane. New York authorities assumed Kahane's assassin, El Sayyid Nosair, was a lone gunman and did not give the case high priority. Nosair was found guilty of a lesser charge.

After the Trade Center bombing, federal authorities examined Nosair's possessions and found evidence of a terrorist conspiracy. They charged Rahman for his role in the Trade Center bombing and for masterminding conspiracies to bomb New York City landmarks and to assassinate Egypt's president. Nine of Rahman's coconspirators were found guilty in the same trial. One of them was Nosair, who was given a life sentence.

Experts disagree as to whether Yousef was a "bomber for hire" or part of a broader terrorist campaign. Many believe he was loosely connected to Muslim fundamentalist groups. Others insist that a terrorist plot as sophisticated as the Trade Center bombing had to have been sponsored by another country. Author Laurie Mylroie believes that Saddam Hussein's intelligence agents planned the attack.

No matter who was ultimately responsible, national-security experts believe that the Trade Center bombing should have put the nation's intelligence community on notice that terrorists were out to kill large numbers of Americans. Some believe that bin Laden and his organization should have been a top national-security priority as early as 1993.

The Trade Center attacks also revealed that federal agencies were not cooperating with one another. The FBI, in particular, resisted turning over evidence because it thought that doing so would jeopardize criminal investigations. That problem persisted for years and is widely considered a reason al Qaeda terrorists were able to succeed on September 11, 2001.

rules is to limit the use of force to legitimate military goals and to protect civilians and other innocent people. Violations, often referred to as war crimes, include mistreating prisoners of war (POWs), using chemical weapons, and bombing civilian targets such as churches and hospitals. Those charged with war crimes can be tried before a military commission rather than a criminal court.

The law of armed conflict allows only "lawful combatants"—those who wear uniforms and carry their weapons openly—to kill others. President Bush takes the position that al Qaeda members and other terrorists are unlawful combatants and therefore candidates for military justice. He finds support in a Supreme Court decision, *Ex Parte Quirin*, 317 U.S. 1 (1942), which upheld the military trials of eight Nazi saboteurs found in the United States during World War II. The Bush administration has declared many of the fighters captured in Afghanistan unlawful combatants and has announced its intention to detain them at the Guantanamo Naval Base in Cuba until the end of the conflict. Some will face military trials. It has also declared two American citizens unlawful combatants because of their ties to the enemy. Like the Guantanamo prisoners, they were placed in military custody until the end of the conflict. In *Hamdi* v. *Rumsfeld*, No. 03-6696 (U.S. Sup. Ct., June 28, 2004), however, the Supreme Court ruled that a detainee had the right to challenge his continued detention.

- **When is it permissible to detain a person who has not been charged with a crime? Should a person be held indefinitely without being charged?**

Unresolved Questions

As the shock of September 11 begins to wear off, some Americans are asking whether their country is taking the right approach toward terrorism. Some believe that the war on terror puts too much emphasis on security at the expense of liberty and that the nation's antiterror effort is setting a bad example for the rest of the world. Others think that the Bush Doctrine is taking the nation's foreign policy in the wrong direction: It is contrary to international law and not in our long-term best interests, and it could make the world more dangerous. At home, some question the president's use of broad wartime powers. They believe some steps taken in past wars were mistakes that should not be repeated and maintain that presidential powers used to fight world wars are not appropriate in a low-level conflict against a small enemy force. Others argue that the post–September 11 antiterror laws make it too easy for authorities to spy on citizens, arrest people without good reason, and mistreat minorities.

- **Has this country become an international bully? Are we losing the respect of the rest of the world?**

Summary

The September 11 attacks marked the beginning of America's war on terror. It is a war in which the enemy is a shadowy organization rather than a hostile country, the objective is hard to define, and fighting could last for years. The United States has responded to the terrorist threat by adopting a new foreign policy under which it will strike first to prevent another attack and by expanding the government's power to find suspected terrorists and bring them to justice. Some Americans believe that the steps taken to fight terror show a lack of respect for the rest of the world and violate traditional American principles of fairness and individual liberty.

The United States Must Act Decisively to Defend Itself

T he Bush Doctrine, under which the United States will strike enemies before they attack and, if necessary, act without international approval, has been criticized both at home and abroad. Defenders of the doctrine maintain that a policy of merely reacting to terrorism leaves us vulnerable to another attack and that protecting Americans deserves a higher priority than does world opinion. They also point out that the United States has a history of taking preemptive military action against other countries.

The Terrorist Threat Requires a New Strategy

After World War II, the United States was engaged in a global struggle, known as the Cold War, with the Soviet Union. At the time, it had a national-security policy based on two principles. One was *deterrence*, building a huge arsenal of nuclear weapons that would be launched at the Soviets if they attacked. The other principle was *containment*, a combination of military, economic, and diplomatic measures to prevent the spread of Communism. Neither the Soviet Union nor the United States wished to start a nuclear war that could destroy all life on Earth. Instead, they indirectly fought one another by supplying arms and other assistance to those fighting in countries such as Afghanistan and Vietnam.

The cold war strategy that kept the Soviets from attacking will not prevent terrorist attacks. As September 11 demonstrated, there are people intent on killing Americans and willing to die in the process. They have also expressed their intention to use weapons of mass destruction against us. Some of those weapons, such as "suitcase nukes," are small enough to be smuggled into this country, hidden until needed, and used without warning. Others, such as missiles carrying atomic warheads, can be launched from thousands of miles away and reach their targets in minutes. As President Bush explained, "America is no longer protected by vast oceans. We are protected from attack only by vigorous action abroad, and increased vigilance at home." [1]

> • **Is the United States doing enough to secure its borders? Is it too easy for foreigners to come in and stay here?**

There Is Both Reason and Precedent for Unilateral Action

In the past, a nation knew when a threat was imminent: A fleet of ships was on its way or troops were massing at the border. Under international law, it was then permissible to take military action. Terrorist cells operate in secret and might be hiding weapons capable of killing more people than an entire squadron of World War II bombers. It is therefore necessary to view the concept of "imminent threat" in a new light. In the words of President Bush, "Facing clear evidence of peril, we cannot wait for the final proof—the smoking gun—that could come in the form of a mushroom cloud." [2]

When President Bush urged military action against Iraq, he reminded Americans of the Cuban missile crisis. In October 1962, American intelligence learned that the Soviet Union had built a nuclear missile site in Cuba. President Kennedy responded to the threat immediately by imposing a naval blockade of Cuba to prevent the Soviets from shipping more weapons. The president explained to the nation why he had to act: "We no longer live in a world where only the actual firing of weapons represents a sufficient challenge to a nation's security to constitute maximum peril. Nuclear weapons are so destructive and ballistic missiles are so swift, that any substantially increased possibility of their use or any sudden change in their deployment may well be regarded as a definite threat to peace."[3]

• When is a terrorist threat "imminent"?

Rather than go to war over the missiles, Soviet Premier Nikita Khrushchev agreed to remove them from Cuba in exchange for Kennedy's promise to take American nuclear weapons out of Turkey.

In 1981, Israel took preemptive action to counter the threat of a nuclear attack. After learning that an Iraqi reactor would soon be able to manufacture plutonium, a radioactive element used in bombs, the Israeli air force destroyed it—even though the Iraqis were years away from making a weapon. Richard Perle, chairman of the Defense Policy Board, argued that Israel faced an imminent threat: "The Iraqis were about to load fuel into the reactor and once they did so, [Israel] would not have had an opportunity to use an air strike without doing a lot of unintended damage around the facility, because radioactive material would have been released into the atmosphere. . . . They had to deal with a threshold that once crossed, they would no longer have the military option that could be effective at that moment."[4]

• Is peace in the Middle East possible? Is the United States treating countries in that region evenhandedly?

It can be argued that the United States faced a similar situation well before September 11. The suicide bombings of two American embassies in August 1998 demonstrated al Qaeda's sophistication and its willingness to inflict mass casualties. Al Qaeda was operating terrorist training camps in Afghanistan, and its leader, Osama bin Laden, had already urged his followers to kill Americans. Many observers believe that, under those circumstances, there was an imminent danger of an al Qaeda attack and that the United States not only had the right to invade Afghanistan but should have done so.

The president's supporters maintain that preemptive military action is nothing new. For more than 200 years, presidents have sent the military to punish countries harboring outlaws, remove dictators from office, and restore order to war-torn nations. In 1983 President Reagan sent a force of Army Rangers and U.S. Marines to Grenada to remove a pro-Communist government from power. Six years later, the first President Bush ordered troops into Panama to arrest dictator Manuel Noriega, who was wanted in the United States on drug-trafficking charges.

- **Is the United States hypocritical when dealing with foreign dictators?**

The United States has also gone to war for humanitarian reasons. Spain's oppression of the Cuban people was one reason for the Spanish-American War, and President Wilson, in asking for a declaration of war against Germany, told Congress he wanted to make the world "safe for democracy." A recent example of a humanitarian war was the 1999 air war by the United States and its North American Treaty Organization (NATO) allies against Serbia. The object of that campaign was to force the Serbian government to stop its campaign of genocide against ethnic Albanians.

- **Should the United States act as the "world's policeman"?**

America Must Be Free to Defend Itself

Supporters insist that the invasion of Iraq was necessary because the United Nations (UN) refused to stop Saddam Hussein from using weapons of mass destruction. They maintain that the UN cannot stand up to rogue countries, in part because its structure is too cumbersome. Under the UN Charter, the 15-member Security Council has to approve military action and each of the Council's five permanent members has veto power. In the case of Iraq, the threat of French and Russian vetoes forced President Bush to organize his own coalition. The stalemate over Iraq also showed that the UN lacks the will to

America's "Small War" Against Terror

Over the years, the United States military has been involved in dozens of low-level operations, the objectives of which have ranged from overthrowing dictators to hunting down bandits. These operations typically involved small numbers of troops and no formal declaration of war. They are sometimes referred to as "small wars."

One of America's earliest small wars was against what modern-day politicians would call state-sponsored terrorists: The Barbary pirates, who targeted American civilians and were supported by hostile governments.

Two hundred years ago, the Barbary States were self-governing provinces of the Turkish Empire. They fought a low-level war against European Christian nations, a war that eventually turned into a protection racket. The Barbary rulers hired pirates to capture ships on the high seas; the ships' crews were held for ransom until payment arrived, and unlucky crewmen were tortured or even sold to slave traders. A number of countries, England in particular, decided it was cheaper to pay tribute to the Barbary rulers in exchange for safe passage than to challenge them.

Once the United States gained its independence from Great Britain, it no longer enjoyed the protection of the Royal Navy. As a result, American shipping became an easy target for the Barbary pirates. In 1793, after 11 merchant ships were seized, President Washington considered military action. After European leaders turned down an American proposal for a naval blockade of the Barbary States, the United States had little choice but to follow their lead and pay tribute. Those payments were a considerable drain on the federal treasury.

enforce its own resolutions. At the time of the invasion, Saddam was in violation of 16 Security Council resolutions going back to 1991, when he agreed to abandon his weapons program and allow UN inspections in exchange for a cease-fire ending the Gulf War. Critics warn that if the UN fails to confront scofflaws like Saddam, it will become irrelevant. President Bush said this happened to the League of Nations in the 1930s: "The League of Nations, lacking both credibility and will, collapsed at the first challenge of the dictators. Free nations failed to recognize, much less confront, the aggressive evil in plain sight. And so dictators went about their business."[5]

Matters came to a head in 1801, when the new president, Thomas Jefferson, adopted a policy that came to be known as "millions for defense, but not one cent for tribute." He ordered the navy to blockade the state of Tripolitania, which was harboring the worst of the pirates. He did so against the advice of his attorney general, who believed that only Congress, not then in session, had the power to declare war. Jefferson was the first of many presidents who believed that he could take military action without congressional approval. A crisis was avoided when Congress authorized him, after the fact, to use "all necessary force" to protect American shipping.

The war with Tripolitania, which was marked by acts of heroism on the part of American seamen, lasted for four years. It ended in May 1805, after a force of Marines and locally recruited Arabs stormed the fortress at Derna and, for the first time, planted the American flag on Old World soil. (The reference to "the shores of Tripoli" in The Marines' Hymn comes from that battle.) The American strategy included overthrowing the pasha of Tripolitania and putting his older brother on the throne—the United States' first attempt at "regime change." The pasha agreed to peace terms before he could be toppled, however.

The peace treaty with Tripolitania did not end America's troubles with the Barbary pirates; attacks persisted for more a decade. After the War of 1812, a combination of diplomacy and threats of naval force persuaded the Barbary States to release their American captives and drop their demands for tribute.

Defenders of the Bush Doctrine also argue that, as the world's only superpower, the United States has a unique responsibility to protect democracy around the world. It inherited that responsibility from Great Britain, which, in the nineteenth century, was the world's mightiest naval power. According to author Max Boot, "Britain battled the 'enemies of all mankind,' such as pirates and slave traders, and took upon itself the responsibility of keeping the world's oceans and seas open to navigation. . . . Britain acted to preserve the balance of power whenever it was endangered, coming to the aid of weak nations (such as Belgium or Turkey) being bullied by the strong (Germany or Russia)."[6] In recent years, the United States has taken the lead in stopping genocide in the former Yugoslavia and battling weapons suppliers and drug traffickers.

> • **Are some countries not ready for democracy? Should we try to impose democracy on them anyway?**

Sometimes we have no choice but to act first. When the costs of taking action are high but the benefits are widely shared—as in the case of eliminating a dangerous dictator—smaller countries are understandably reluctant to make the first move. In those situations, it becomes our responsibility to mobilize the rest of the world. Another problem is that other countries do not take the threat of terrorism as seriously as we do. Richard Perle remarked, "I would be surprised if someone over coffee and apple cake in Oslo would feel similarly threatened. So we shouldn't expect our European friends and allies to share the sense of apprehension that we have as a result of September 11th."[7]

> • **Have the September 11 attacks caused our government to act too hastily?**

The strongest argument in favor of the Bush Doctrine is national sovereignty: It is unacceptable for unelected foreign bureaucrats to control America's foreign policy. As Vice President

Dick Cheney explained, "To accept the view that action by America and our allies can be stopped by the objection of foreign governments that may not feel threatened is to confer undue power on them, while leaving the rest of us powerless to act in our own defense."[8]

The president's supporters insist that the United Nations has no business dictating our foreign policy: The UN Charter does not trump the Constitution, which obligates the president, as commander-in-chief of the armed forces, to provide for the common defense. They are also disturbed by a trend toward world government, which they think will do more harm than good. Their biggest concern is that international bodies will regulate American military power, reducing the president's ability to defend us from dictators and aggressors. Scholars David Rivkin and Lee Casey warn, "If the trends of international law in the 1990s are allowed to mature into binding rules, international law will prove to be one of the most potent weapons ever deployed against the United States."[9] Some even foresee the day when hostile regimes will try to prosecute American military commanders, even the president himself, on trumped-up charges of war crimes.

- **Is a world government possible? Would it be an improvement over the world's current governments?**

Sometimes Force Is the Best Option

Diplomacy is usually preferable to war, but there are times when attacking an enemy is less dangerous than continuing to negotiate. One of history's most famous examples of diplomatic failure was European leaders' efforts to appease Adolf Hitler. In 1938, Hitler demanded that a portion of Czechoslovakia called the Sudetenland be handed over to Germany. Great Britain, France, and Italy agreed to give Hitler the Sudetenland in exchange for his promise not to demand any more territory. Afterward, British Prime Minister Neville Chamberlain said he had brought "peace in our time." Chamberlain was wrong. Hitler took over the rest of Czechoslovakia and later invaded Poland, forcing the Allies to go to war to stop him. In the months leading up to the invasion of Iraq, President Bush compared Saddam Hussein to Hitler and warned that unless

Bringing War Criminals to Justice

International criminal law has existed for centuries, but until recently, only countries were believed to have the power to punish violators. That notion changed after World War II. As the war neared an end, the Allies debated what to do with Adolf Hitler and other top Nazi officials. British Prime Minister Winston Churchill favored executing them all. The United States proposed an alternative: trying the Nazis for war crimes before an international court. American officials believed that trials would identify the guilty individuals and expose their crimes to the world. The other Allies agreed to create an international tribunal to try alleged war criminals.

The tribunal, which consisted of judges from France, Great Britain, the Soviet Union, and the United States, met in Nuremberg, Germany, the city where the Nazis held their party rallies and enacted the notorious racial classification laws. In November 1945, the first trial began. It focused on major war criminals (lower-ranking officials were tried later). The defendants were charged with traditional violations of the law of armed conflict as well as two new offenses, "crimes against peace" and "crimes against humanity," which are now recognized in international law. The trials were governed by procedures that in many ways resembled those used in American criminal cases, although there was no jury trial and no appeal.

In October 1946, after hearing more than 200 days of testimony, the judges returned their verdicts. They found 19 defendants guilty and sentenced 12 to death, 3 to life in prison, and 4 to lesser prison terms. They found 3 not guilty. The judges rejected the argument that only a state, and not an individual, could be guilty of war crimes. They also rejected the argument that a person was not guilty if he was only following orders, a plea now called the "Nuremberg defense." Legal experts generally believe that the Nuremberg trials were fair, although it can be argued that some of the charges were ex post facto, meaning that actions were defined as crimes after the fact. Like other war crimes trials, Nuremberg has been criticized as "victor's justice": No Allied leaders were tried for war crimes.

Saddam were removed from power he would become an even greater menace in the years to come.

- **Which is the bigger threat to this country, foreign dictators or terrorist organizations?**

Afterward, some members of the United Nations proposed a permanent Nuremberg-style war crimes tribunal; the Cold War stalemate between the United States and Soviet Union prevented its creation. In 1993, the UN Security Council created a special tribunal to prosecute those responsible for "ethnic cleansing" and other war crimes in Bosnia. It was the first such court to prosecute a head of state, former Yugoslav president Slobodan Milosevic, and also the first to recognize rape as a war crime. The Security Council later established another tribunal to prosecute war crimes committed in Rwanda.

In 1998, delegates at a UN-sponsored conference in Rome voted overwhelmingly in favor of creating a permanent International Criminal Court with jurisdiction over cases of genocide, crimes against humanity, and violations of the law of armed conflict. The treaty took effect July 1, 2002.

The International Criminal Court is a "court of last resort," one that may act only when the country with primary responsibility either cannot or will not prosecute. It is aimed at regimes such as Pol Pot's in Cambodia, where there was no independent justice system. Supporters of the court believe that a permanent institution is less likely to dispense victor's justice because the list of offenses has been drawn up in advance and the judges and prosecutors are already in place.

Nevertheless, the United States is concerned that members of its armed forces, which are stationed in more than 100 countries around the world, could become targets of politically motivated prosecutions for war crimes. It voted against creating the court and has asked its allies and the UN Security Council to give American service members immunity from prosecution.

Supporters of the court believe that American fears are exaggerated, pointing out that there are safeguards against unfair prosecutions and that Americans charged with war crimes can be tried here under our system of military justice. They add that, by rejecting the court's jurisdiction, the United States will find itself in the company of such rogue nations as Burma, Cuba, and North Korea.

Saddam Hussein is no longer in power, but there are other dictators who oppress their people and support terrorist groups. Many believe that a show of strength is the only way to force them to cooperate. They also contend that retreating after an attack—pulling American troops out of Lebanon after a Marine barracks there was bombed, for example—sends a message that terrorism works. According to Middle East scholar Reuel Marc Gerecht, "Without a militant America to inspire (and worry) them, foreign liaison services will act in their rulers' best interests, which when dealing with bin Ladenesque radicalism will mean ignoring the Americans as much as possible." [10]

Gerecht cites the example of Pakistan, whose president, Pervez Musharraf, not only backed the Taliban regime but also relied on "graduates" of al Qaeda's training camps to fight against India. After September 11, Secretary of State Colin Powell warned Musharraf to renounce terrorism or else face the consequences. Musharraf abandoned the Taliban, fired pro-Taliban officers from the army and intelligence service, and confronted Pakistani militants he had previously supported. The president's supporters also point to Iraq as proof that military force works. They argue that Saddam's downfall frightened Libyan dictator Muammar Gadafi into abandoning his weapons of mass destruction and Iran's regime into allowing weapons inspectors into their country.

> • **Does invading Muslim countries create more radicals like Osama bin Laden?**

Summary

The most important responsibility a country owes its citizens is defense. The September 11 attacks forced the United States to shift its national security strategy from retaliating after an attack to preventing one in the first place. Supporters of the Bush Doctrine believe that international organizations like the United Nations are neither able nor willing to confront dictators. They insist that the United States has a unique responsibility to fight terrorism and protect human rights and that other countries' attempts to control our military power will encourage terrorists and enable dictators to defy the rest of the world.

Unilateralism and Preemptive War Do More Harm Than Good

America's war on terror began with broad international support: The North Atlantic Treaty Organization (NATO) declared that the September 11 attacks were attacks on all of its members, and the United Nations Security Council unanimously passed a resolution supporting "international efforts to root out terrorism" in Afghanistan,[1] approving in principle the American-led invasion. More recently, though, the United States has been at odds with much of the world over its foreign policy, especially for waging a preemptive war against Iraq without UN approval.

> • **Do international organizations have too much control over American policy?**

The Iraq war is part of a larger controversy surrounding the Bush Doctrine, which emphasizes both unilateral and preemptive military action. Critics believe that such a policy will create even worse problems than those the Bush administration is trying to solve.

The Bush Doctrine Raises Legal and Ethical Concerns

After World War II, world leaders tried to prevent future wars by establishing international rules restricting the use of force. The Nuremberg trials recognized aggression—going to war without justification—as a war crime, and the United Nations Charter, which the United States signed, obligated its members to use force only in self-defense.

> • **Were the news media evenhanded in their coverage of the Afghanistan and Iraq wars?**

Some believe that, by leading an invasion of Iraq, the United States abused its right to defend itself. The Defense Department defines a *preemptive war* as "an attack initiated on the basis of incontrovertible evidence that an enemy attack is imminent," and a *preventive war* as one "initiated in the belief that military conflict, while not imminent, is inevitable, and that to delay would involve greater risk."[2] A preemptive war is generally considered legitimate, but a preventive war is not; in fact, some find it hard to distinguish a preventive war from *aggression*. Some experts believe that the Iraq war was preventive because Saddam Hussein did not pose an imminent threat to the United States. Before the war, a panel of New York City lawyers found that "Iraq has not, since the end of the 1991 Gulf War, used force or directly threatened the United States (aside from attacks on allied airplanes in the no-fly zones). Logically, any threat that Iraq poses is not of an immediate nature."[3]

Finally, the Bush Doctrine increases the risk of going to war on a mistaken assumption. Even though American forces captured Saddam Hussein, they still have not found his weapons of mass destruction—the principal reason for going to war against Iraq.

• **Did the president exaggerate the threat Iraq posed to this country? Was he the victim of faulty intelligence?**

Unilateral Military Action Makes the World More Dangerous

A foreign policy that relies on military power and seeks regime

FROM THE BENCH

When Can the President Wage War?

The framers of the Constitution, who did not want the United States to be ruled by a king, divided war powers between the president and Congress. Article II, §2 of the Constitution makes the president commander-in-chief of the military, but Article I, §8, Clause 11 gives Congress the power to declare war.

The lack of a clear dividing line between presidential and congressional powers has led to long-running political debate, as well as occasional lawsuits to stop pending wars (a war does not require a formal declaration: only five American wars were ever declared). Presidents have contended that the commander-in-chief power is broad enough to go to war without congressional approval. Many lawmakers and legal scholars believe the framers of the Constitution intended to limit the president's war-making power to "repelling sudden attacks." So far, the courts have avoided facing the issue head-on, citing a number of reasons why it would be inappropriate to act. Cases from recent wars include these:

Massachusetts v. Laird, 451 F.2d 26 (1st Cir. 1971). A federal appeals court found that Congress effectively approved the Vietnam War by repeatedly voting to keep funding it. As a result, the court found that Congress and the president had not taken opposite positions on the war, leaving no clear issue to decide.

Dellums v. Bush, 752 F. Supp. 1141 (D.D.C. 1990). A federal district court rejected a challenge to the Gulf War because the issue was not yet "ripe": The president had not made a final decision to go to war, and Congress had yet to vote on a resolution authorizing military force (it would pass such a resolution days before the war began).

Doe v. Bush, 323 F.3d 133 (1st Cir. 2003). A federal appeals court refused to stop the invasion of Iraq, finding that no "case or controversy" had arisen because last-minute diplomacy still could avert war. The court suggested change overseas could leave the world—the United States included—more dangerous in the long run. Some believe that the Bush Doctrine will encourage other countries to speed up their nuclear weapons programs in an effort to ward off an American invasion. International lawyers David Rivkin and Lee Casey explain, "Ultimately, the 'right of humanitarian intervention' is not likely to produce a more just and safe world,

---

that a case or controversy might exist if Congress gave the president a "blank check" to wage war or if the president ordered military action in defiance of a congressional resolution.

The dispute between branches of government is further complicated by the War Powers Resolution (50 U.S.C. §§1541–1548), which Congress passed over President Richard Nixon's veto in 1973. The act requires the president to notify Congress within 48 hours after taking military action and requires congressional approval if the campaign lasts longer than 60 days. Nixon, and the presidents who followed him, believed that this resolution was unconstitutional but nevertheless acted consistently with its requirements.

So far, the courts have avoided ruling on the resolution's constitutionality. In Campbell v. Clinton, 203 F.3d 19 (D.C. Cir. 2000), some members of Congress sued President Clinton for allegedly violating the War Powers Resolution by continuing the Kosovo war past the 60-day deadline. The Court of Appeals refused to decide the case, ruling that Congress still had legislative means of ending the conflict, such as ordering an end to the war or refusing to approve funds for it. It added that Congress had sent a mixed message about Kosovo: The House voted to fund operations there and defeated a resolution ordering the president to end the war immediately.

According to legal commentator John Dean, "Scholars agree that Campbell v. Clinton largely ended all hope of using the federal courts to hold the president accountable under a constitutional requirement that Congress must declare or authorize war before a president can engage in war."* Dean pointed out, however, that Congress can stop a war by cutting off funding; it did so in 1974, forcing President Nixon to end America's involvement in Vietnam.

* John W. Dean, "Pursuant to The Constitution and Despite Claims to The Contrary, President Bush Needs Congressional Approval Before Declaring War on Iraq," FindLaw.com, August 30, 2002. Available online at http://writ.news.findlaw.com/dean/20020830.html.

but to impel vulnerable states to obtain weapons of mass destruction as a means of preventing Western intervention in their internal affairs."[4] Professor Michael Ignatieff of the Carr Center for Human Rights Policy at Harvard University adds, "To date, the only factor that keeps the United States from intervening is if the country in question has nuclear weapons. . . . No wonder a Pakistani general is supposed to have remarked in 1999 that the chief lesson he drew from the display of American precision air power in Kosovo was for his country to acquire nuclear weapons as quickly as possible."[5]

There is also concern that America's policy of preemptive military action might encourage other countries to attack their long-time enemies. India and Pakistan have gone to war several times in the past and recently came close to fighting another war over the disputed territory of Kashmir. North Korea has threatened to attack South Korea. China has threatened to invade Taiwan if it declares its independence. All of those potential aggressors have nuclear weapons.

• **Is the U.S. military stretched too thin? Should we increase the size of our armed forces?**

Critics of the Bush Doctrine worry that, although preemptive military action might pay short-term dividends, it creates serious problems in the long run. Richard Falk, a professor of international law at Princeton Unversity, warns that the fight against terror "is a war in which the pursuit of the traditional military goal of 'victory' is almost certain to intensify the challenge and spread the violence."[6] One likely consequence of invading another country is a guerrilla war—a lesson the Soviets learned in Afghanistan. Another consequence is terrorism. Since the Vietnam War, extremists around the world have portrayed the United States as an imperialist power and thus a legitimate target of terrorism. Bill Christison, a former senior CIA officer, explains, "Whatever the military success of the U.S. . . . a couple of years hence new extremists just as clever as bin Laden, and hating the U.S. even more, will almost certainly arise somewhere else in the world. That's why we need to understand the root causes behind the terrorism."[7]

> • **Are we doing enough to win the "hearts and minds" of Arabs and Muslims?**

Some believe that relying on military force to fight terrorism plays into the hands of Osama bin Laden, who seeks to portray his fighters as *jihadi*, or holy warriors, against modern-day Crusaders. Sir Michael Howard, a prominent military historian who has taught in Great Britain and the United States, believes that we should learn from Great Britain's long experience with terrorists: "In the intricate game of skill played between terrorists and the authorities, as the British discovered in both Palestine and Ireland, the terrorists have already won an important battle if they can provoke the authorities into using overt armed force against them. They will then be in a win-win situation: either they will escape to fight another day, or they will be defeated and celebrated as martyrs."[8]

America Has Become a Bad International Citizen

The Bush Doctrine has added to a perception overseas that the United States has become a law unto itself. Since the end of the Cold War, this country has increasingly defied the rest of the world, rejecting the Convention on the Rights of the Child, the Law of the Sea Treaty, the Kyoto Protocol on global climate change, the Anti-Landmine Convention, and, especially, the International Criminal Court. The United States not only voted against creating the court, but also considers it illegitimate and has taken steps to defeat its jurisdiction. Many believe that, by walking away from the court, the United States wasted its chance to persuade other countries to improve it.

Critics also accuse the United States of inconsistency in its dealings with international bodies. The International Court of Justice (World Court) is one example. After the 1979 Iranian

Revolution, this country obtained a judgment condemning Iran's holding of American hostages. Later, however, the United States argued the World Court had no jurisdiction to hear Nicaragua's complaint that American forces mined its harbors. Some believe that such behavior sets a bad example, encouraging other countries to ignore their international commitments as well.

- **Should the United States obey orders handed down by the World Court? Is the idea of a World Court unworkable?**

Critics believe that, by ignoring the international community, the United States has not only squandered the world's sympathy toward it—the French newspaper *Le Monde* ran the famous headline, "We Are All Americans," after September 11—but also inflamed anti-American sentiment, especially in the Middle East. In 2003, a Pew Research study found that foreigners' attitudes toward the United States had become strongly negative since the September 11 attacks. Anti-American feeling might, in the long run, encourage other countries to form alliances aimed at keeping this country in check.

Finally, ignoring allies costs money. Professor Ignatieff observes, "Where US interventions have had perceived legitimacy and coalition support—in Bosnia, Kosovo and Afghanistan—the US has been able to share burdens, transfer costs and begin to plan an exit. In Iraq, it will bear the costs mostly alone, without an exit in sight." [9] In the 1991 Gulf War against Iraq, the United States acted with UN approval and persuaded its allies to contribute most of the cost that war. In contrast, the only country that made a significant military commitment to the 2003 war was Great Britain, and America's traditional allies, including France and Germany, have been reluctant to supply troops or contribute financial aid toward Iraq's reconstruction.

Some argue that the war also drained funds from what ought to be the nation's first priority: preventing another terrorist attack. Professor Jeffrey Record of the U.S. Air Force's Air War College explains, "Homeland security is probably the greatest [global war on terrorism] opportunity cost of the war against Iraq. Consider, for example, the approximately $150 billion already authorized or requested to cover the war and postwar costs (with no end in sight). This figure exceeds by over $50 billion the estimated $98.4 billion shortfall in federal funding of emergency response agencies in the United States over the next five years." [10]

> • **Was Saddam's removal enough of a reason to go to war? Should we go to war to remove other dictators from power?**

America Still Needs Allies

The United States is the world's only superpower, but it is still in our long-term best interest to work with the rest of the world to fight terror as well as other national-security threats such as global warming and infectious diseases. Professor Ignatieff believes the United States has forgotten that reality: "It is dependent on Mexico and Canada to keep its border secure; it needs Europe's police forces to track terrorist cells in the Islamic diaspora. It cannot contain the North Korean nuclear threat without the Chinese, Japanese and South Koreans. Preventing the Pakistani regime from collapsing and its nuclear weapons from falling into terrorist hands depends on the cooperation of the Indian government." [11] He also warns, "Without friends and allies, a war against terror will fail." [12]

After World War II, the United States and its allies benefited from working together. Notable successes include the United Nations; the Marshall Plan, which helped rebuild Europe; and NATO, which contained the Soviet Union. They made allies of former enemies and set the stage for victory in the Cold War.

A foreign policy that stresses overseas intervention—especially in the pursuit of loosely defined goals such as fighting terror and promoting democracy—creates the risk that the United

States will overextend itself, the same mistake that led to the fall of the Roman Empire. Military experts warn that the American military is already overstretched by fighting simultaneous wars in Afghanistan and Iraq and against terrorists worldwide.

- **Should Americans take the threat of terrorism more seriously? Should we make greater sacrifices to defeat it?**

Finally, the international community has come to the realization that "nonstate actors" such as drug cartels, arms proliferators, and terrorists threaten global security. In fact, the UN has taken steps in the fight against terror. After the September 11 attacks, the Security Council passed Resolution 1373, one of its strongest ever. This resolution calls on member countries to crack down on terrorists inside their borders and to make it illegal to provide financial aid to terrorist organizations. Although the UN is unpopular with many Americans, it is highly regarded overseas and can open doors the United States cannot. In fact, some Islamic countries, as well as the Association of Southeast Asian Nations (ASEAN), have said that they will take part in a campaign against terrorism only if it is carried out under UN leadership.

THE LETTER OF THE LAW

Use of Force: Article 51 of the UN Charter

Nothing in the present Charter shall impair the inherent right of individual or collective self-defence [sic] if an armed attack occurs against a Member of the United Nations, until the Security Council has taken measures necessary to maintain international peace and security. Measures taken by Members in the exercise of this right of self-defence shall be immediately reported to the Security Council and shall not in any way affect the authority and responsibility of the Security Council under the present Charter to take at any time such action as it deems necessary in order to maintain or restore international peace and security.

- **Is the United Nations capable of settling international disputes? Should it concentrate instead on humanitarian projects?**

Summary

The Bush Doctrine, which contemplates unilateral American action, even without the approval of other countries, has alienated much of the world and might violate international law. The doctrine also makes the world more dangerous by encouraging countries to invade their neighbors and acquire nuclear weapons and by breeding terrorist organizations. The doctrine is also self-defeating. As powerful as the United States is, it still needs allies to combat terrorism and other security threats. Our refusal to abide by international treaties and work with bodies such as the UN could lead other countries to not cooperate with, or even to oppose, American efforts to fight terrorism.

Military Justice Is an Appropriate Way to Deal With Terrorists

After September 11, 2001, the United States and its allies took thousands of enemy fighters into custody. Most surrendered or were captured during the invasion of Afghanistan, but others were apprehended by intelligence and law-enforcement agencies. The president declared hundreds of them unlawful combatants, an action he maintained was consistent with the law of armed conflict and court decisions from past wars. He also argued that it was legal not only to detain unlawful combatants indefinitely but also to try those accused of war crimes before military commissions.

- Should an accused terrorist receive the same due process of law as an accused drug dealer?

46

America Is at War

Legal experts agree that the September 11 attacks—the mass murder of civilians by enemy fighters disguised as civilians— were an act of war. Many believe that al Qaeda had been at war with the United States as early as 1998, when Osama bin Laden advocating killing Americans and his followers bombed American embassies in Africa.

> • **Should we have invaded Afghanistan before September 11? Should we have tried to assassinate Osama bin Laden?**

After the September 11 attacks, the United States went to war. Congress did not formally declare war, but it did pass a resolution authorizing the president to take military action against those responsible for the attacks. Even though the war on terror differs from past conflicts, the president has the same constitutional duty as other wartime presidents: to provide for the common defense. Because he is the commander-in-chief of the armed forces, it is ultimately his decision where to send troops, how to attack the enemy, and what to do with enemy fighters who surrender or are captured. In past conflicts, the courts refused to substitute their judgment for that of the president. Chief Justice Harlan Stone once stated, "The war power of the national government is 'the power to wage war successfully.'. . . It extends to every matter and activity so related to war as substantially to affect its conduct and progress. The power is not restricted to the winning of victories in the field and the repulse of enemy forces."[1]

> • **Has the president been unfairly second-guessed about his handling of the fight against terrorism?**

There are good reasons for courts to defer to the president's military judgment. Wartime decisions must be made swiftly, often on the basis of incomplete or conflicting information, and the president is accountable to voters, while judges are

(continued on page 50)

Military Commissions and the Constitution: Ex Parte Milligan and Ex Parte Quirin

During the Civil War, military authorities arrested thousands of civilians living in the North on charges of disloyalty to the Union government. Many were tried by military commissions.

In 1864, a Union spy uncovered a plot by Southern sympathizers to stage an uprising in Indiana. Lamdin Milligan and four alleged coconspirators were arrested, tried by a military commission, and sentenced to death. Although President Andrew Johnson commuted their sentence to life in prison, they filed a habeas corpus petition in federal court. Habeas corpus, a centuries-old legal check on governmental abuse of power, allows a person in custody to ask a court to determine whether he is being detained lawfully. In this case, Milligan and his codefendants argued that a military commission had no authority to try them.

The case reached the Supreme Court, which, in Ex Parte Milligan, 71 U.S. 2 (1866), ordered the prisoners' release. All nine justices agreed that the Bill of Rights was not suspended in wartime and that the prisoners should not have been tried by a commission. They disagreed on the reason for their decision, however. Justice David Davis, writing for the five-member majority, concluded that a military trial was unconstitutional under the circumstances: Milligan and his fellow defendants were not in the armed forces, and Indiana was neither in a state of rebellion nor under invasion by the Confederate army. Even though the Habeas Corpus Act of 1863, which authorized the government to detain accused criminals without charging them, was constitutional, military justice was not:"Martial rule can never exist where the courts are open, and in the proper and unobstructed exercise of their jurisdiction. It is also confined to the locality of actual war."

Four justices, led by Chief Justice Salmon Chase, agreed with the result. However, they believed that the case should have decided on a narrower issue and therefore wrote a concurring opinion. It concluded that the government violated the Habeas Corpus Act by not freeing Milligan and his fellow defendants after the Indiana grand jury finished its term without charging them with any crimes. The concurring justices also suggested that there might come a time when Congress would determine that civilian courts were not capable of hearing cases involving national security:"Those courts might be open and undisturbed in the execution of their functions, and yet wholly incompetent to avert threatened danger, or to punish, with adequate promptitude and certainty, the guilty conspirators."

The Supreme Court did not revisit the issue of military trials until World War II, when federal authorities arrested eight Nazi agents who had been sent to the United States to commit sabotage. The defendants filed a habeas corpus petition alleging that the government had no authority to try them before a commission. Their case quickly reached the Supreme Court, which, in Ex Parte Quirin, 317 U.S. 1 (1942), unanimously upheld the constitutionality of their military trial. Chief Justice Harlan Stone found that the Articles of War, passed by Congress, authorized trials by commission for violators of the law of armed conflict. In this case, after the men came ashore in the United States, they took off their German military uniforms and put on civilian clothes. By fighting without wearing "fixed and distinctive emblems," they became violators. The Court stated:

> Lawful combatants are subject to capture and detention as prisoners of war by opposing military forces. Unlawful combatants are likewise subject to capture and detention, but in addition they are subject to trial and punishment by military tribunals for acts which render their belligerency unlawful. The spy ... or an enemy combatant who without uniform comes secretly through the lines for the purpose of waging war by destruction of life or property, are familiar examples of belligerents who are generally deemed not to be entitled to the status of prisoners of war, but to be offenders against the law of war subject to trial and punishment by military tribunals (emphasis added).

Stone also rejected the argument that American citizens could not be tried by commissions: "Citizenship in the United States of an enemy belligerent does not relieve him from the consequences of a belligerency which is unlawful because in violation of the law of war."

In addition, the chief justice concluded that Ex Parte Milligan did not bar military trials in this case, explaining that Lamdin Milligan, "not being a part of or associated with the armed forces of the enemy, was a non-belligerent, not subject to the law of war."

One issue left open by Quirin is whether the president, as commander-in-chief of the armed forces, has the inherent power to try enemy fighters before a commission. That issue is likely to arise when accused terrorists face trials before President Bush's military commissions.

(continued from page 47)

not. When new enemies such as al Qaeda confront us, it is important that the president be given flexibility in deciding how to fight them. A federal appeals court recently stated, "As the nature of threats to America evolves, along with the means of carrying out those threats, the nature of enemy combatants may change also. In the face of such change, separation of powers doctrine does not deny the executive branch the essential tool of adaptability." [2]

> • **Should the president have broad war powers? Is there a danger he might become a dictator?**

Detaining Enemy Fighters Is a Legitimate Wartime Measure

Although the invasion of Afghanistan was in many ways a conventional war, al Qaeda is a new kind of enemy: Its members fight for a cause, not for a specific country, and they carry out acts of terrorism while living among their victims. Al Qaeda fighters have also repeatedly violated the law of armed combat by attacking civilians, not wearing identifying insignia, and not carrying their weapons openly. Like the saboteurs in *Quirin*, they are unlawful combatants who can be tried by a military commission for war crimes.

> • **Are war crimes a form of revenge on the losing side? Can "victor's justice" be eliminated?**

The U.S. military detained more than 600 alleged enemy combatants at Guantanamo. Some either have been, or will be, charged with war crimes and will face trials before military commissions. Additionally, the Bush administration detained at least two Americans as unlawful combatants. Although the Supreme Court ruled that detainees can challenge their status, the administration still maintains that it has the power to detain enemy combatants until the end of the conflict with al Qaeda.

- **Should the Guantanamo detainees have been given a day in court? Should those not charged with war crimes be freed?**

Indefinite detention of enemy combatants is a preventive measure, not punishment. If they are freed, they might rejoin al Qaeda and commit more acts of terrorism against Americans. Their detention is also specifically permitted by international law. Lawyers David Rivkin and Lee Casey point out:

> The right to detain captured enemy combatants, without trial, without lawyers and without an established release schedule, stems from one of the most important humanitarian advances in the law of armed conflict, dating back at least to the 17th century—the rise of an obligation to "give quarter." Before this, except for a few wealthy or powerful individuals worth ransoming, captured soldiers could be, and very often were, put to the sword.[3]

The military also believes that some detainees have valuable intelligence about al Qaeda activity and has been interrogating them in an effort to stop future terrorist attacks.

- **Should we be humane toward those who lack respect for our human rights? Toward those who have vowed to kill Americans?**

The Bush administration insists that it is up to the president, not the courts, to decide which detainees are unlawful combatants and that the status of enemy fighters is the very kind of decision courts refused to question in past conflicts. But in *Hamdi* v. *Rumsfeld*, the Supreme Court balanced the president's commander-in-chief power and a citizen's right to due process. It allowed a detainee to challenge his unlawful-combatant status, but it ruled that such a challenge could be heard by a military panel.

Even before the Supreme Court ruled that the Guantanamo detainees had the right to challenge their detention, the Defense

Department created a panel that would review each detainee's case on a regular basis and make an independent recommendation to the Defense Department.

The Criminal Justice System Cannot Deal With Terrorism

The September 11 attacks were acts of war. For that reason, experts such as former White House lawyer Bradford Berenson insist, "A person making war on the U.S. who seeks to slaughter thousands of our citizens in the streets must face our military, not our judges."[4] They stress that there is

THE LETTER OF THE LAW

Rules of Procedure in Military Commission Trials

After President Bush created military commissions to try suspected terrorists, civil liberties groups and some lawmakers objected. In March 2002, the Defense Department issued an order that clarified the rules governing trials before military commissions.*

Section 5 of the order provides a number of safeguards for the accused, including the following:

- Written notice of the charges
- The presumption of innocence until proven guilty
- The requirement that guilt be proved beyond a reasonable doubt
- The right to a defense lawyer before and during the trial
- Access to the prosecution's evidence, including evidence that could prove innocence
- The right to remain silent
- The right to testify
- The right to call witnesses and obtain documents
- The right to present evidence and cross examine prosecution witnesses

a difference between fighting a war and pursuing common criminals. No one believes that American troops need a warrant to search Osama bin Laden's cave or that they must give captured al Qaeda fighters their Miranda warnings before questioning them.

There are several reasons why the criminal justice system cannot deal effectively with terrorism. First, it focuses on punishing criminals after the fact; thus, it is not well-suited for preventing terrorist acts. The possibility of imprisonment, or even the death penalty, does not deter a hijacker who is willing to become a martyr to his cause. In addition, the

- The services of an interpreter, if one is needed
- The right to be present at the trial
- The right to make a statement and present evidence on the issue of sentencing
- A guarantee against being tried twice for the same offense

Section 6 of the order provides the following additional safeguards:

- The accused will be given a "full and fair trial."
- Irrelevant evidence may not be admitted.
- The trial will be open except when necessary to ensure national security.
- A guilty verdict requires a two-thirds vote of the commission, and a death sentence requires a unanimous vote.
- A guilty verdict may be reviewed by a military review panel. The secretary of defense may reduce a verdict to a lesser offense and may reduce a sentence.

* U.S. Department of Defense, Draft Military Commission Order No. 1. Washington, D.C.: U.S. Department of Defense, 2002. Available online at http://www.defenselink.mil/news/Mar2002/d20020321ord.pdf.

purpose of a criminal trial is to decide whether an individual is guilty or innocent, not to evaluate and react to threats to national security. Author Laurie Mylroie commented on the trials after the first World Trade Center attack, "The American public mistook the 'guilty' verdicts for an explanation of the bombing."[5]

The rules that govern criminal trials also make them inappropriate for dealing with terrorists. First of all, the standard of guilt—proof beyond a reasonable doubt—might be too high for the government to meet. Laurie Mylroie explains, "That high standard has a purpose. It aims to protect the life, liberty, and property of U.S. citizens against abuse by authority. But that is not the standard that is used in national security affairs. It never could be, because such certainty rarely exists."[6]

- **Have we struck the right balance between individual liberty and public safety?**

Intelligence agencies must act on the basis of doubtful evidence, sometimes even on a hunch. If they have to work under the same restrictions as the police, they might not be able to stop terrorists from attacking. Bradford Berenson observes, "At the point of apprehension, we may not know what a terrorist is planning, his plans may not yet have ripened into prosecutable crimes."[7]

The rules of criminal procedure can keep important evidence from being introduced. One example is the hearsay rule, which prevents statements by nonwitnesses from being used as evidence. Ruth Wedgwood, a law professor at Yale University, provides an example: "[Osama] bin Laden's telephone call to his mother, telling her that 'something big' was imminent, could not be entered into evidence if the source of information was his mother's best friend."[8]

Another example is the exclusionary rule, which bars the use of evidence gathered in violation of the Constitution. As a result, a confession offered by a person who was not given Miranda warnings could not be used as evidence, even if it identified specific terrorists and set out the details of a terrorist plot. Rules such as these make it more likely that terrorists will be set free, only to commit more acts of terror.

> • **Do the courts make it too easy for accused criminals to go free? Should we let accused terrorists take advantage of legal technicalities?**

Furthermore, the government's evidence against accused terrorists might include military secrets that cannot be disclosed in the courtroom or details of government investigations, such as which terrorist cells have been infiltrated. Even the disclosure of seemingly harmless information can be damaging. During the embassy bombing trial, it was revealed that American intelligence had intercepted Osama bin Laden's satellite phone conversations. Bin Laden stopped using his satellite phone, and the United States lost him. There is also the possibility that a terrorism trial could become a media circus or, even worse, could be used by someone like bin Laden to spread his radical views to the rest of the world.

Finally, criminal trials are expensive and time consuming. The two trials that arose out of the 1993 World Trade Center bombing lasted for months and involved hundreds of witnesses and a vast amount of evidence. Elaborate precautions had to be taken to keep terrorists from intimidating or retaliating against the judge and jury.

> • **The September 11 attacks have been likened to Pearl Harbor. Is that comparison valid?**

Military Justice Is a Recognized Means of Dealing With War Criminals

In *Quirin*, the Supreme Court noted that military justice has been recognized for centuries; in fact, the law of

(continued on page 58)

FROM THE BENCH

Can Civilian Courts Try Terror Suspects?
United States v. Moussaoui

Advocates of military justice believe that United States v. Moussaoui shows why criminal trials are not appropriate for accused terrorists. The case began in August 2001, when Zacarias Moussaoui, a French citizen, raised the suspicions of his instructors at a Minnesota flight school when he expressed an interest in flying jumbo jets and in simulating a flight from London to New York. The instructors alerted the FBI, which detained Moussaoui on immigration charges.

After the September 11 attacks, investigators found evidence linking Moussaoui to the 19 hijackers. At first, federal authorities suggested that he was the "twentieth hijacker" who never made it aboard United Airlines Flight 93, which crashed in Pennsylvania. Moussaoui denied involvement in September 11, even though he admitted belonging to al Qaeda. Nevertheless, a federal grand jury in Virginia indicted him on six counts of conspiring with the September 11 hijackers. Four counts carried the death penalty.

Moussaoui's trial was bogged down when the defense team demanded access to Ramzi bin al-Shibh, an al Qaeda figure who allegedly helped plan the September 11 attacks and whose testimony might clear Moussaoui of any role in the hijacking conspiracy. The lawyers argued that without bin al-Shibh's testimony, Moussaoui could not get a fair trial as guaranteed by the Sixth Amendment.

The government argued that in cases like Moussaoui's, national security overrides the accused's right to obtain favorable testimony. It pointed out that al-Shibh had been captured overseas and was being held as an enemy combatant and contended that making him available would interfere with his interrogation and hamper efforts to learn about future al Qaeda attacks.

John Yoo, a law professor at the University of California, Berkeley, warned that a ruling in Moussaoui's favor could cripple future terrorism cases: "Like Moussaoui, [accused terrorists] will call for access to every al-Qaeda terrorist in U.S. custody somewhere in the world. It will be terrorism graymail, and the government will be very vulnerable to it."* In fact, lawyers for John Walker Lindh, the "American Taliban," reportedly demanded access to al Qaeda leaders. Lindh's case was settled by a plea bargain before the issue could be ruled on.

After the government refused to produce bin al-Shibh, Moussaoui's lawyers asked the judge to sanction, or penalize, the government for violating their client's rights. The judge found that the government had acted improperly and, in addition, that Moussaoui was a "remote or minor participant" in al Qaeda's plans. She stopped short of dismissing the charges against Moussaoui. Instead, she barred the government from seeking the death penalty or telling the jury that Moussaoui had any involvement in, or knowledge of, the September 11 attacks.

The judge's ruling presented the government with a difficult decision. If it appealed, it faced the possibility of an unfavorable ruling that would leave it with a much weaker case. On the other hand, if it dropped criminal charges and tried Moussaoui before a military commission, civil-liberties groups would accuse it of "forum shopping"—looking for the court most likely to hand down a favorable judgment—and the public might think it never had a strong case.

The government chose to appeal, believing that it had a good chance of persuading the Fourth Circuit, considered the nation's most conservative appeals court, that it had a strong argument for not making bin al-Shibh available. In April 2004, the appeals court gave the government most, but not all, of what it asked for. It allowed the government to introduce evidence that linked Moussaoui to the September 11 attacks and to seek the death penalty, but it ordered the trial court to work out a compromise under which summaries of al Qaeda prisoners' testimony could be presented to the jury. Moussaoui's lawyers have appealed the ruling, and the case may end up before the Supreme Court.

Meanwhile, there is disagreement surrounding Moussaoui's role in the September 11 hijackings. The independent panel investigating September 11 found "good reason to believe" that, when he was taken into custody, he was under consideration as a replacement for one of the pilots.

---

* Philip Shenon, "Judge Rules Out a Death Penalty for 9/11 Suspect," The New York Times, October 4, 2003.

(continued from page 55)

armed conflict and the use of military commissions to try violators are both older than the Constitution. The United States used commissions to try Major John André, caught spying for the British during the Revolutionary War; those

THE LETTER OF THE LAW

Crimes Triable Before a Military Commission

In March 2002, the Defense Department issued a draft instruction listing the crimes that can be tried before a military commission.[*]

Section 3 of the order states that the crimes are derived from the law of armed conflict. The list is not comprehensive because military commissions follow the "common law of war," meaning that new offenses can be recognized as international standards of acceptable wartime conduct change. In Application of Yamashita, 327 U.S. 1 (1946), the Supreme Court upheld a Japanese military commander's conviction of a newly created offense: failing to prevent his troops from committing atrocities.

Section 6 lists the elements of specific crimes, including the following:

- Willful killing of "protected persons" (soldiers, chaplains, and medics)

- Attacking civilians

- Attacking civilian property that is not part of the enemy's war-making capability

- Attacking protected property (churches, hospitals, and museums)

- Pillaging (seizing property for personal use)

- Issuing a "take no prisoners" order when enemy forces are in a position to surrender unconditionally

- Taking hostages

- Using chemical or biological weapons

- Using protected persons as "human shields"

- Improper use of a flag of truce

- Improper use of protective emblems (the Red Cross, for example) who conspired with John Wilkes Booth to assassinate President Lincoln and other high officials; and German and Japanese officials accused of atrocities during World War II.

- Rape

- Hijacking

- Terrorism. There are five elements to the offense:

  (1) Killing, inflicting great bodily harm, or destroying property

  (2) Done either intentionally or with "wanton disregard" for life

  (3) Intended to intimidate or coerce a civilian population, influence a government's policy, or affect a government's conduct

  (4) Carried out by someone other than a lawful combatant, or against a nonmilitary target

  (5) In the context of and associated with armed conflict

- Aiding the enemy (providing arms or money, harboring enemy fighters, or giving information to the enemy)

- Spying

The order also applies to those who aid and abet violators, attempt or conspire to commit a crime, order others to commit a crime, or protect violators from being apprehended. In addition, a commanding officer can be held responsible for crimes committed by subordinates if he fails to take reasonable steps to stop them or does not report violators to the proper authorities.

* U.S. Department of Defense, Draft Military Commission Instruction: Crimes and Elements for Trials by Military Commissions. Washington, D.C.: U.S. Department of Defense, 2003. Available online at http://www.defenselink.mil/news/Feb2003/d20030228dmci.pdf.

Supporters of military commissions reject the charge that they are "kangaroo courts" in which the outcome is known in advance. They point out that President Bush's commissions will provide the accused with more legal protection than the commission that tried the *Quirin* defendants. In an effort to provide a "full and fair hearing," the accused will be represented by a military lawyer, will have the right to call and cross examine witnesses, and may choose to remain silent. A death sentence will require a unanimous vote, and a guilty verdict can be reviewed by a military appeals panel. It has also been suggested that military trials are fairer because judges are likely to make their judgment based on the facts alone. Former federal appeals court Judge Robert Bork explains, "Military judges tend to be more scrupulous in weighing evidence, in resisting emotional appeals, and in respecting the plain import of the laws. There are no Lance Itos or Johnny Cochrans in military trials."[9] Nor do military courts automatically convict. At the Nuremberg trials, the judges found some Nazi leaders not guilty and gave others lighter sentences.

- **Have military commissions become a relic of the past? Are they biased against the accused?**

- **If Osama bin Laden is caught, who should try him? An international court? An American military commission? A federal criminal court?**

Summary

The president, as commander-in-chief of the armed forces, is entitled to considerable leeway in waging war, including the treatment of captured enemy fighters. The current war on terror is no exception. Both the law of armed conflict and national-security considerations justify President Bush's decision to detain hundreds of fighters as unlawful combatants. The same considerations justify his use of military commissions instead of civilian courts to try accused terrorists. Because of restrictive rules of evidence and the requirement of proof beyond a reasonable doubt, civilian trials pose too great a risk that accused terrorists will go free. The use of commissions has long been recognized by international law, and they provide swift justice and, at the same time, fairness to the accused.

The War on Terror Violates Human Rights

E ven during wartime, presidential power is not absolute. Chief Justice of the Supreme Court William Rehnquist describes the laws as "muted" but not silent, and court decisions from past conflicts suggest that there is a limit somewhere. Critics believe that President Bush's indefinite detention of captured enemy fighters and his creation of military commissions to try war criminals went beyond the president's war powers. Even if those measures were acceptable in past wars, they are contrary to modern notions of fairness and violate internationally recognized standards of human rights.

> • Is "war" the right word to describe the fight against terrorism? Do you think our country is on a war footing?

The Fight Against Terror Is Not a War

Not everyone believes that the president's power as commander-in-chief of the armed forces justifies the indefinite detention of enemy fighters and the use of military commissions to try terrorists. Some, like Professor Anne-Marie Slaughter, dean of Princeton's Woodrow Wilson School of Public and International Affairs, question whether the president's claim to broad wartime power is appropriate: "The insistence that we are 'at war' also justifies extraordinary measures that would be unthinkable in ordinary time. In fact, the size and scale of our campaign in Afghanistan is much closer to our military campaigns in Kosovo, Bosnia, or Somalia—all specific and limited 'missions.'" [1]

Critics believe that the fight against terror is really a large-scale police operation that will be won through international cooperation and painstaking investigative work, not through military action. Professor Michael Howard prefers the British approach of treating terrorism as an "emergency." During an emergency, "the police and intelligence services were provided with exceptional powers and were reinforced where necessary by the armed forces, but they continued to operate within a peacetime framework of civilian authority." [2]

> • **Is the government abusing the antiterror laws? Might it do so in the future?**

America's Treatment of the Enemy Raises Questions

Even assuming we are at war, some believe that the president has gone beyond the limits of his commander-in-chief power. They maintain that he had no legal basis for declaring the Guantanamo detainees unlawful combatants and denying them prisoner-of-war status and the rights that go with it, such as sending and receiving mail, living in the same quality housing as Americans on the base, and freedom from the intensive interrogation reportedly taking place.

- **How far should our military go in questioning those who know about terrorist activity?**

Some experts believe that the *Quirin* decision, which the Bush administration relies on as authority for treating al Qaeda and Taliban fighters as unlawful combatants, misinterpreted international law. Although the law of armed combat requires a fighter to wear "fixed and distinctive emblems" and "carry arms openly," his failure to do so does not automatically make him an unlawful combatant. Diane Orentlicher and

FROM THE BENCH

The Rights of Guantanamo Detainees: Rasul v. Bush

After the invasion of Afghanistan, the United States military classified more than 600 captured al Qaeda and Taliban fighters as "enemy combatants" and transferred them to Guantanamo Naval Base in Cuba. Some detainees insisted that they were innocent people caught in the "fog of war" and should not be detained. For more than two years, they were denied their day in court.

The reason was Johnson v. Eisentrager, 339 U.S. 763 (1950), a Supreme Court decision that arose out of World War II. In 1945, American forces in China arrested 21 German nationals caught helping the Japanese after Germany unconditionally surrendered. They were tried before a military commission in China, given prison terms, and transferred to an American military base in Germany to serve their sentences. The prisoners filed a habeas corpus petition challenging their military trials. By a 6–3 vote, the Supreme Court refused to consider their petitions. The Court rejected the argument that the Constitution "followed the flag," concluding instead that the Fifth Amendment's guarantee of due process did not apply to noncitizens captured and detained on foreign soil. As a result, the prisoners could be "deprived of liberty by Executive action without hearing."

Despite the Eisentrager decision, 16 Guantanamo detainees filed habeas corpus petitions challenging their indefinite detention without being charged with a crime or given an opportunity to challenge their enemy-combatant status. In al-Odah v. United States, 321 F.3d 1134 (D.C. Cir. 2003), the Court of Appeals for the District of Columbia Circuit ruled that the detainees' petitions should be dismissed because they were not American citizens and Guantanamo was outside

Robert Goldman, law professors at American University, explain, "At the time *Quirin* was rendered, a combatant who failed to distinguish himself as required by customary law did not thereby violate the laws of war, *although his specific hostile acts may have* (emphasis added)." [3]

In other words, only a small minority of those detained at Guantanamo were unlawful combatants liable to be tried for war crimes. Some experts raise an additional argument, namely, that the term "unlawful combatant" appears nowhere in the Geneva Conventions, and accuse the Bush

---

the sovereign territory of the United States. In reaching its decision, the appeals court rejected the argument that Guantanamo should be considered American territory. It concluded that a 1903 lease agreement with Cuba gave the United States control, but not sovereignty, over Guantanamo.

In Rasul v. Bush No. 03-334 (U.S. Sup. Ct., June 28, 2004), however, the Supreme Court concluded by a 6–3 majority that federal courts did have jurisdiction to hear the detainees' petitions. It sent the case back to the District Court with instructions to decide whether the detainees should be released.

Justice John Paul Stevens wrote the majority opinion. He concluded that this case was distinguishable from Eisentrager for several reasons. First, the Guantanamo detainees denied taking arms against the United States but were never given a chance to show their innocence. In addition, Court decisions after Eisentrager had made it easier for those detained outside a federal court's territorial jurisdiction to sue for habeas corpus. Furthermore, it was clear that the United States had jurisdiction over Guantanamo Naval Base. Finally, the detainees had alleged that they were being held in federal custody in violation of American law.

Justice Antonin Scalia dissented. He maintained that the habeas corpus law did not apply to noncitizens detained outside the sovereign territory of the United States and that there was no difference between this case and Eisentrager. He added that the majority's decision would allow courts to second-guess the president's decisions relating to war.

administration of illegally creating a category of second-class military prisoners.

> • **Is the United States being "two-faced" on the issue of human rights?**

Critics also accuse the Bush administration of two other violations of the Geneva Conventions: refusing to convene a "competent tribunal" to determine the status of enemy fighters and not treating them as POWs pending a decision by the tribunal. Until the Supreme Court ruled against it, the Bush administration classified all of the Guantanamo detainees as unlawful combatants. Still, the Bush administration stands by its blanket determination that all of the Guantanamo detainees were unlawful combatants and maintained that the courts lacked power even to review its determination.

> • **Should the courts second-guess how the president wages war? Are they a necessary check on the abuse of presidential power?**

Even if the Constitution gives the president final authority to decide who is an unlawful combatant, his doing so could result in a miscarriage of justice. Former Vice President Al Gore contends, "Now if the President makes a mistake, or is given faulty information by somebody working for him, and locks up the wrong person, then it's almost impossible for that person to prove his innocence—because he can't talk to a lawyer or his family or anyone else and he doesn't even have the right to know what specific crime he is accused of committing."[4]

Critics also point out that the Bush administration's treatment of enemy fighters is contrary to American policy in past conflicts. In both the Vietnam War and the Gulf War, the military set up tribunals to determine the status of captured enemy fighters. Those critics also accuse the Bush administration of having tried to create a legal "black hole" by holding the detainees under military control and arguing that the base was beyond the reach of federal courts.

Military Justice Is Unfair

Opponents of President Bush's military commissions believe that the commissions are unconstitutional. They criticize the *Quirin* decision as a product of wartime overreaction by the courts, like the now-discredited decisions upholding the constitutionality of the government's forced relocation of Japanese Americans to internment camps.

Even if *Quirin* is good law, critics maintain that the president's military order goes beyond the boundaries of that decision. The order authorizes military trials not only for those responsible for the September 11 attacks, but also for terrorists in general—and even those who aided, abetted, or harbored terrorists. A task force of leading American lawyers found "it is not clear that membership, alone, in al Qaeda or harboring terrorists violates the law of war" and that "not all acts of international terrorism are necessarily violations of the law of war."[5] It is therefore possible that a person who has not committed a war crime could find himself before a military commission. Furthermore, it is not clear whether President Bush had the authority to create commissions in the first place. The *Quirin* Court left open the question of whether the president could create commissions without congressional authorization.

- **When does a crime of violence become terrorism? Does it depend on intent? On the death and destruction involved?**

Even if using military commissions to try terrorists is constitutional, opponents argue that the commissions fall short of internationally recognized standards of fairness. Diane Orentlicher and Robert Goldman explain, "Human rights instruments binding on the United States mandate that criminal defendants, whatever their offenses, be tried by independent and impartial courts that afford generally recognized due process guarantees. By their very nature, military commissions do not satisfy this basic test."[6]

A number of commission procedures raise questions of fairness. The standard for charging someone—"reason to believe" that a person has committed a war crime—is lower than that in criminal cases. The judges and the lawyers for both sides are military officers who belong to the same chain of command, raising the possibility of pressure from higher-ups to reach a guilty verdict. Commissions have broad leeway in deciding what evidence to consider, including evidence that could not be used in criminal trials, and how much weight to give that evidence. A guilty verdict requires only a two-thirds vote. Finally, decisions are reviewed by a military appeals panel, and civilian court review is extremely limited. Given the stakes involved—commissions can order the death penalty—the risk of convicting an innocent person is unacceptably high.

Mistreatment of Enemy Fighters Hurts America's Image

Human-rights groups complain that enemy fighters detained at Guantanamo have been mistreated. According to the Center for Constitutional Rights, "The United States has denied the [Guantanamo] detainees access to counsel, consular representatives, and family members, has failed to notify them of the charges they are facing, has refused to allow for judicial review of the detentions, and has expressed its intent to hold the detainees indefinitely. Meanwhile, the United States has continued to interrogate the prisoners."[7]

> • **Is our treatment of the Guantanamo detainees setting a bad example for the rest of the world?**

Critics warn that the Bush administration's treatment of the detainees has damaged America's reputation abroad. Some accuse it of being hypocritical by condemning other countries for trying their political opponents before military commissions while proposing to do the same to alleged terrorists. Others fear that America's violating human-rights standards in the name of fighting terror will lead to a worldwide "race to the bottom." International lawyer John Whitbeck explains:

> Not surprisingly, since September 11, virtually every recognized state confronting an insurgency or separatist movement has eagerly jumped on the "war on terrorism" bandwagon, branding its domestic opponents (if it had not already done so) "terrorists" and, at least implicitly, taking the position that, since no one dares to criticize the United States for doing whatever it deems necessary in its "war on terrorism," no one should criticize whatever they now do to suppress their own "terrorists."[8]

Our actions also create the risk that other countries will retaliate against Americans abroad, including those serving in the armed forces. Al Gore warns, "If we don't provide [POW treatment to detainees], how can we expect American soldiers captured overseas to be treated with equal respect? We owe this to our sons and daughters who fight to defend freedom in Iraq, in Afghanistan and elsewhere in the world."[9]

Finally, recognizing a "terrorism exception" to the rule of law could lead to a gradual erosion of our civil liberties. Journalist Edwin Dobb argues that "civil rights lose their legitimacy, their claim on our conscience, as soon as any one person is excluded from their protection."[10]

- **Are war crimes trials fair? Should heads of state be put on trial for war crimes?**

There Are Alternatives to Military Justice

Human-rights groups not only objected to the Bush administration's treatment of the Guantanamo detainees but also condemned its intention to hold them until the war on terror is over. Had the Supreme Court not ruled in the detainees' favor, they could have been detained for the rest of their

(continued on page 72)

FROM THE BENCH

Detaining Americans as "Enemy Combatants": Hamdi v. Rumsfeld and Padilla v. Rumsfeld

After the September 11 attacks, two American citizens—Yaser Hamdi and José Padilla—were apprehended, declared "enemy combatants," and detained indefinitely. The circumstances surrounding their capture were different, but both men raised the same argument: They were denied the right to challenge their detention in court.

Hamdi was captured on the battlefield during the American-led invasion of Afghanistan. He was declared an enemy combatant and eventually confined in a military prison in South Carolina. His father filed a habeas corpus petition, which the U.S. Court of Appeals for the Fourth Circuit dismissed in Hamdi v. Rumsfeld, 316 F.3d 450 (4th Cir. 2003). The appeals court concluded that the declaration of a Pentagon official, which stated that Hamdi was fighting with a Taliban unit and had an AK-47 assault rifle in his possession, was enough evidence to justify the president's decision to detain him.

Hamdi's father appealed to the Supreme Court. In Hamdi v. Rumsfeld, No. 03-6696 (U.S. Sup. Ct., June 28, 2004), eight justices concluded that Hamdi's continued detention was unconstitutional. Justice Sandra Day O'Connor wrote the majority opinion. She concluded that if Hamdi were in fact an enemy combatant, the law of armed combat not only authorized his initial detention but also his being held until the fighting in Afghanistan ended. But she also concluded that due process of law entitled Hamdi to challenge his enemy-combatant status before a neutral decision maker. Justice O'Connor found that due process did not require a court hearing governed by the usual rules of evidence; a military panel operating under proper rules could hear Hamdi's appeal. She also found that due process required giving Hamdi the opportunity to rebut the government's evidence that he was an enemy combatant. She observed, "An interrogation by one's captor, however effective an intelligence-gathering tool, hardly constitutes a constitutionally adequate factfinding before a neutral decisionmaker."

Justices Antonin Scalia and David Souter also concluded that Hamdi should be released, but for different reasons. Justice Scalia argued that, because habeas corpus had not been suspended, the government had no power to detain Hamdi indefinitely; its only two options were to charge him with a crime against the state or set him free. Justice Souter contended that Hamdi should be set free because a 1971 act of Congress, the Anti-Detention Act, barred the president from detaining American citizens without clear congressional authorization.

Justice Clarence Thomas dissented, arguing that Congress's use-of-force resolution gave the president the power to detain enemy combatants. He added that, because the president's military judgments should be deferred to, due process required only a good-faith determination of Hamdi's status—even if it was mistaken.

Unlike Hamdi, Padilla was arrested inside the United States after flying home from Pakistan. He was originally jailed in New York in connection with a criminal investigation of the September 11 attacks. Shortly afterward, President Bush declared him an enemy combatant. The president alleged that al Qaeda had sent Padilla to the United States to scout out locations where terrorists could detonate a "dirty bomb," a makeshift weapon capable of dispersing radioactive material. Padilla was turned over to the military, transferred to a naval prison in South Carolina, denied the opportunity to meet with family members or his lawyer, and subjected to ongoing questioning about his links to terrorists. He was never charged with an offense.

Padilla's attorney filed a habeas corpus petition in U.S. District Court in New York. The case went to the U.S. Court of Appeals for the Second Circuit, which, in Padilla v. Rumsfeld, 352 F.3d 695 (2d Cir. 2003), ordered him released from military custody. The appeals court concluded that the president could not detain an American citizen seized on American soil and outside a combat zone as an enemy combatant. It found that Padilla's detention was outside the president's commander-in-chief power and was not authorized by an act of Congress. The government appealed to the Supreme Court.

In Rumsfeld v. Padilla, No. 03-1027 (U.S. Sup. Ct., June 28, 2004), a 5–4 majority ruled that Padilla's lawyer had filed her client's habeas corpus petition in the wrong court. It dismissed her petition and told her to file a new one in South Carolina. In his majority opinion, Chief Justice William Rehnquist concluded that the commandant of the naval prison where Padilla was held, not Defense Secretary Donald Rumsfeld, had "immediate custody" over Padilla and that only the South Carolina court had jurisdiction over the commandant.

Justice John Paul Stevens dissented, calling Padilla's case "exceptional" because he was declared an enemy combatant and taken to South Carolina after he was jailed in New York and assigned a lawyer there. Justice Stevens also maintained that it was proper to name Secretary Rumsfeld as a party because he had been personally involved in the decision to have Padilla detained. He also denounced open-ended detention for the purpose of interrogation, suggesting that it was a form of torture.

(continued from page 69)

lives without being charged with a crime or given a chance to show they were wrongly held. Ronald Dworkin, a law professor at New York University, has suggested a two-month time limit for deciding whether to classify a detainee as a prisoner of war or a potential war criminal and recommends releasing a prisoner of war after three years, by which time any intelligence he might offer has become stale.

Legal experts also have suggested alternatives to military commissions. One is an international tribunal, similar to that used at Nuremberg, to try leading al Qaeda figures; some suggest inviting judges from Islamic countries to take part so the trials will not be seen as Western persecution of Muslims.

Another suggestion, made by a panel of New York City lawyers, is to try accused war criminals by court-martial rather than before a commission: "Military courts-martial . . . combine an essentially non-jury trial in a secure environment— a naval vessel or military base—pursuant to established rules of procedure, evidence and appeal based on written records. The due process provided in these courts is genuine, despite the old adage about military justice and military music, even while the trial process is made more efficient than in civilian courts."[11]

Finally, some believe that civilian courts can and should be used to try low-level terrorists, as well as those who aided terrorist organizations by committing crimes such as money laundering. As a panel of New York City lawyers found, "American courts have tried international criminals who have violated the law of nations—including pirates and slave traders—since the beginning of the nation. We have convicted hijackers, terrorists and drug smugglers."[12]

- **Should terrorists be tried by an international tribunal? Should those who killed Americans face American justice?**

Supporters of civilian trials believe that there are ways to ensure security, such as keeping cameras out of the courtroom, protecting the identity of jurors and witnesses, and severely punishing those who disclose sensitive information.

Summary

Critics dispute whether the war on terror is really a "war" and, even if it is, whether it justifies the broad use of presidential powers. They maintain that the president has no legal authority to declare enemy fighters "unlawful combatants," detain them indefinitely, or try terrorists before military commissions. Even where the treatment of enemy fighters is constitutional, critics warn that it violates international human-rights standards, puts this country in a bad light, and invites other countries to commit similar violations.

New Laws Are Needed to Fight Terrorism

Attorney General John Ashcroft said that the September 11 attacks taught us that terrorists had outflanked law enforcement in technology, communications, and information, making it necessary for the government to have new legal tools to fight for Americans' life and liberty.

The Patriot Act, which passed overwhelmingly in both houses of Congress, provides those tools. Contrary to what critics claim, "Congress simply took existing legal principles and retrofitted them to preserve the lives and liberty of the American people from the challenges posed by a global terrorist network."[1]

- **Could our government have prevented the September 11 attacks? What steps should it have taken?**

The Terrorist Threat Requires New Legal Tools

After the September 11 attacks, America retaliated against al Qaeda by leading an invasion that destroyed its training camps and killed or captured much of its leadership. Military force alone, however, cannot defeat al Qaeda, whose members dress as civilians and live among us. The fight requires law-enforcement and intelligence work at home.

As criminals became more sophisticated, law-enforcement agencies were given new legal tools to deal with them. Al Qaeda presents threats of even greater magnitude: It intends to kill thousands of Americans and it is difficult for law-enforcement agencies to infiltrate. For those reasons, police and prosecutors need the same legal weapons to fight terrorism that they have to fight drug lords and crime syndicates. As Senator Joseph Biden argued during floor debate on the Act, "The FBI could get a wiretap to investigate the Mafia, but they could not get one to investigate terrorists. To put it bluntly, that was crazy! What's good for the mob should be good for terrorists."[2]

• **Has the war on terror made the government too big and powerful? Has it caused the erosion of civil liberties?**

Today, those weapons are available. For example, Section (§) 206 of the Patriot Act allows authorities to use "roving wiretaps," which apply to any phone or computer a suspected terrorist might use. The use of roving wiretaps has been legal in drug investigations since 1986. Section 220 of the act allows courts to issue nationwide search warrants, a court-approved law-enforcement tool that is needed to keep up with highly mobile terrorists who use multiple cell phones and send e-mail from libraries and Internet cafés.

The Patriot Act also updated the federal criminal code. It created new terror-related offenses, such as harboring terrorists and unlawful possession of a biological weapon; imposed longer prison terms on convicted terrorists; and eliminated the statute of

Tapping in and turning up the heat

Among other effects, the Patriot Act of 2001 broadened law enforcement's ability to investigate crimes using electronic means:

- Payment information of e-mail and Internet customers, such as credit card or bank account numbers, can be obtained with a subpoena.

- E-mail and Internet service providers are permitted to disclose customer records to law enforcement in cases of an emergency involving immediate risk of death or serious physical injury.

- Non-content information, such as e-mail addresses and Internet addresses, can be identified with a subpoena in the same way phone numbers of incoming and outgoing calls are identified.

Wiretap applications

Government requests for wiretap authority are rarely denied by judges.

Year	Authorized	Denied
1990	922	0
1991	941	0
1992	966	0
1993	1,182	0
1994	1,200	0
1995	1,139	0
1996	1,197	1
1997	1,276	0
1998	1,443	2
1999	1,521	0
2000	1,190	0
2001	1,491	0

SOURCES: U.S. Department of Justice; Center for Democracy & Technology   AP

As criminals become more sophisticated, new legal tools are needed to deal with them. The 2001 Patriot Act gave law-enforcement agencies the ability to investigate crimes using electronic means, as described in the chart above.

limitations for crimes involving terrorism. The act also gave the Treasury Department new powers to disrupt the financing of terrorist organizations and made it easier for the Justice Department to detain and deport noncitizens who have links to terrorists.

Most important, the Patriot Act seeks to remove a serious obstacle to catching terrorists: the "wall" separating domestic law enforcement from foreign intelligence gathering. The wall was created in the 1970s, after it was revealed that the government spied on thousands of political opponents, including Dr. Martin Luther King, Jr. Stewart Baker, who served as legal counsel to the National Security Administration (NSA), explains, "That 'wall'—between intelligence and law enforcement—was put in place to protect against a hypothetical risk to civil liberties that might arise if domestic law enforcement and foreign intelligence missions were allowed to mix. It was a post-Watergate fix meant to protect Americans, not kill them."[3]

- **Have political leaders exploited the September 11 attacks for political gain?**

Like many government officials, Baker once believed that the wall was a good idea because "foreign intelligence gathering tolerates a degree of intrusiveness, harshness, and deceit that Americans do not want applied against themselves."[4] That wall was well intentioned, but it hampered the government's ability to stop terrorists. In fact, Baker thinks it grew so high that it might have prevented authorities from stopping the September 11 attacks. In the days leading up to the attacks, the government knew that two of the hijackers, Khalid al-Mihdhar and Nawaf al-Hazmi, were in the United States but could not locate them. Had they been found, the other hijackers might have been tracked down. An FBI intelligence agent in New York who was looking for al-Mihdhar and al-Hazmi asked the Bureau's criminal investigators for help in finding them. His higher-ups turned him down, telling him that criminal information could not be passed over the wall. The intelligence agent responded with the following email: "some day someone will die—and wall or not—the public will not understand why we were not more effective and throwing every resource we had at certain 'problems.' Let's hope the [lawyers who gave the advice] will stand behind their decisions then, especially since the biggest threat to us now, UBL [Usama Bin Laden], is getting the most 'protection.'"[5]

- **Before September 11, did the United States underestimate the threat of terrorism?**

Section 203 of the Patriot Act specifically allows law-enforcement and foreign-intelligence personnel to share information. Many legal experts believe that this provision was not just necessary but overdue because it makes little sense to draw fine legal distinctions between crime and terrorism in dealing with an enemy like al Qaeda.

Critics Exaggerate the Dangers of Antiterror Laws

William Rehnquist, the chief justice of the Supreme Court, observed, "The laws will thus not be silent in times of war, but they will speak with a somewhat different voice."[6] As a wartime measure, the Patriot Act is modest compared with those of past conflicts. It does not affect basic rights such as habeas corpus and the presumption of innocence in criminal trials, and courts continue to oversee searches carried out by law-enforcement agencies. There have been some civil-liberties violations under the act, but they are not systematic, as they were when President Lincoln used military commissions to punish his critics or when the military interned Japanese Americans during World War II.

- **How does the fight against terror resemble wars of the past? In what ways does it differ?**

Supporters of the Patriot Act believe that it has been unfairly criticized. They complain that critics have focused on a handful of controversial provisions and read them out of context to create the impression that the government has been given dangerous new powers. One example is §213 of the act, which allows law-enforcement agencies to search a person's property without first notifying him. Critics call it the "sneak-and-peek" provision and suggest that it breaks new legal ground. Delayed notification is nothing new, however. Some

(continued on page 81)

THE LETTER OF THE LAW

Major Provisions of the Patriot Act

After the September 11 attacks, Congress passed the "Uniting and Strengthening America by Providing Appropriate Tools Required to Intercept and Obstruct Terrorism" ("USA-Patriot") Act (Public Law 107-56). It is a complex piece of legislation that amended numerous provisions of the United States Code.

The act's most controversial provisions deal with government surveillance. Overall, these provisions widen the scope of searches and lower the standard the government must meet to monitor people. Some surveillance provisions apply to criminal investigations in general; others apply to "foreign intelligence" investigations, which focus on the activities of agents of foreign powers, including suspected terrorists. Foreign-intelligence searches are governed by the Foreign Intelligence Surveillance Act (FISA), which created a secret court that hears applications for them. Because national security is at stake, it is easier for the government to get authorization for a FISA search. Because FISA court does not ask the government to justify requests for surveillance, critics argue that it offers no protection against abuses.

Major provisions of the act include the following (those governing FISA searches are marked with an asterisk):

§203. Makes it easier for law-enforcement agencies to share foreign intelligence gathered in a criminal investigation with other federal agencies.

§206*. Permits "roving wiretaps," which apply to any phone or computer surveillance target might use, including computers at public facilities.

§209. Allows the government to get a court order to seize voice mail as well as e-mail messages.

§213. Allows a law-enforcement agency to execute a search warrant without first notifying the person searched. The agency must show a court that notification would cause an "adverse result."

§214*. Makes it easier to use pen registers and trap and trace devices in foreign-intelligence investigations.

§215*. Authorizes court orders directing third-party holders of business records—such as financial, medical, or library records—to turn them over to the government if they are relevant to a terrorism investigation.

§216. Imposes clearer standards for government monitoring of Internet use. A court order is required, and the content of online communications— as opposed to email addresses or URLs of Websites—may not be monitored.

§218*. Expands the government's power to gather foreign intelligence. To carry out surveillance, the government must show the court that foreign intelligence information is "a significant purpose," rather than "the purpose," of the search.

§220. Allows federal courts to issue nationwide search warrants for electronic evidence such as email communications.

§223. Increases the civil liability of a person who unlawfully discloses information obtained through a search and requires administrative discipline for officials guilty of unlawful disclosure.

§224. Provides that a number of Patriot Act provisions automatically expire on December 31, 2005.

§411. Authorizes the Justice Department to deport a non–U.S. citizen who associates with a terrorist organization.

§412. Authorizes the detention of a noncitizen for up to seven days without being charged if the person is a danger to national security. Allows detention beyond the seven-day period if the person is deportable and release would endanger national security.

§501. Authorizes the Justice Department to offer cash rewards for information about terrorism.

§503. Requires persons convicted of a terrorism offense or any violent crime to provide a sample for the national DNA database.

§505. Authorizes the FBI to issue a "national security letter" directing a holder of business records to turn them over. The FBI must certify that the records are relevant to an ongoing terrorism investigation and that the person whose records are asked for is an "agent of a foreign power." In September 2004, a federal court in New York found this section unconstitutional.

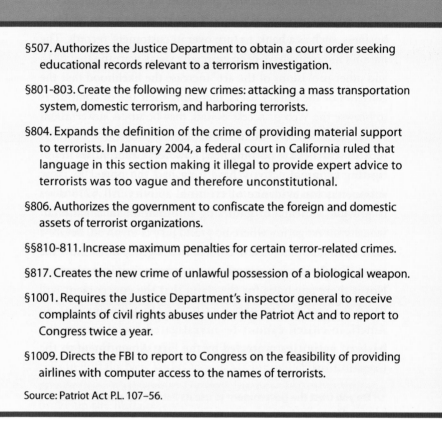

§507. Authorizes the Justice Department to obtain a court order seeking educational records relevant to a terrorism investigation.

§801-803. Create the following new crimes: attacking a mass transportation system, domestic terrorism, and harboring terrorists.

§804. Expands the definition of the crime of providing material support to terrorists. In January 2004, a federal court in California ruled that language in this section making it illegal to provide expert advice to terrorists was too vague and therefore unconstitutional.

§806. Authorizes the government to confiscate the foreign and domestic assets of terrorist organizations.

§§810-811. Increase maximum penalties for certain terror-related crimes.

§817. Creates the new crime of unlawful possession of a biological weapon.

§1001. Requires the Justice Department's inspector general to receive complaints of civil rights abuses under the Patriot Act and to report to Congress twice a year.

§1009. Directs the FBI to report to Congress on the feasibility of providing airlines with computer access to the names of terrorists.

Source: Patriot Act P.L. 107–56.

(continued from page 78)

time ago, courts recognized that there were circumstances in which the police could search first and notify the owner afterward—when the person might flee, destroy evidence, or kill or intimidate witnesses after learning that a search was about to take place. Critics of §213 also fail to mention that a delayed-notification search requires a warrant and that a court will authorize one only if the government can show that notification would jeopardize the investigation.

- **Should the government track our travel and spending habits? Should it monitor the websites we visit?**

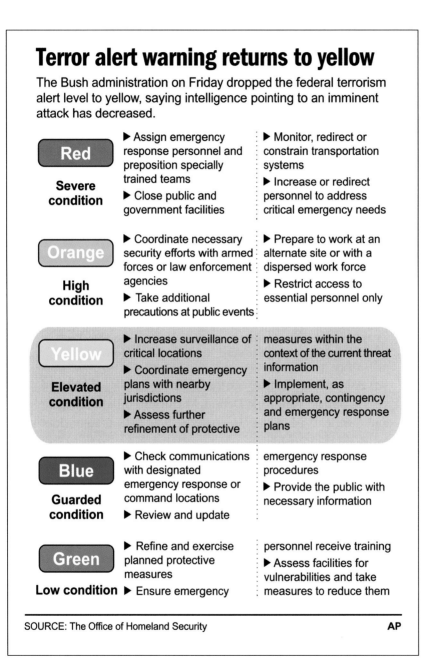

Terror alert warning returns to yellow

The Bush administration on Friday dropped the federal terrorism alert level to yellow, saying intelligence pointing to an imminent attack has decreased.

Red

Severe condition

▶ Assign emergency response personnel and preposition specially trained teams
▶ Close public and government facilities

▶ Monitor, redirect or constrain transportation systems
▶ Increase or redirect personnel to address critical emergency needs

Orange

High condition

▶ Coordinate necessary security efforts with armed forces or law enforcement agencies
▶ Take additional precautions at public events

▶ Prepare to work at an alternate site or with a dispersed work force
▶ Restrict access to essential personnel only

Yellow

Elevated condition

▶ Increase surveillance of critical locations
▶ Coordinate emergency plans with nearby jurisdictions
▶ Assess further refinement of protective

measures within the context of the current threat information
▶ Implement, as appropriate, contingency and emergency response plans

Blue

Guarded condition

▶ Check communications with designated emergency response or command locations
▶ Review and update

emergency response procedures
▶ Provide the public with necessary information

Green

Low condition

▶ Refine and exercise planned protective measures
▶ Ensure emergency

personnel receive training
▶ Assess facilities for vulnerabilities and take measures to reduce them

SOURCE: The Office of Homeland Security   **AP**

The Office of Homeland Security uses a color-coded system, as in the chart above, to designate federal terrorism alert levels.

to cut their prison time by pleading guilty and cooperating with the government.[10]

The Justice Department also credits the Patriot Act for the arrests of Sami al-Arian, the alleged American leader of Palestinian Islamic Jihad, a terrorist group responsible for murdering more than 100 people, including a young American woman killed in Gaza, and Hemant Lekhani, an alleged arms dealer charged with attempting to sell shoulder-fired missiles to terrorists for use against American targets such as passenger jets.

Finally, Americans favor the Patriot Act. In a July 2003 FOX News/Opinion Dynamics poll, 55 percent considered the Patriot Act "a good thing for America," despite the criticism it had gotten; 91 percent believed that the act has not affected their civil liberties. The war on terror has had a minor effect on everyday life; Americans rarely notice stepped-up security except when they go to the airport or attend a concert or sporting event.

- **Do you think al Qaeda still poses a threat to America? Could there still be al Qaeda "sleeper cells" here?**

Liberty Is Impossible Without Security

Supporters of the Patriot Act maintain that it was not a hasty overreaction to September 11 but rather a comprehensive and balanced response to terrorism. They emphasize that the purpose of government is not only to safeguard citizens' freedom but also to protect their lives, and they point out that "there is no more basic civil liberty than the right not to be blown to bits."[11] Even assuming that parts of it are flawed, they insist the Patriot Act is better than the alternative:

> Imagine what would happen if the war against terrorism fails. Repeated attacks would create panic, and a terrible backlash against civil liberties would ensue. As the casualty toll grew, the calls for Draconian measures would make

Congressional Authorization for the Use of Military Force Against the Perpetrators of September 11

Public Law 107-40 (Senate Joint Resolution 23)

To authorize the use of United States Armed Forces against those responsible for the recent attacks launched against the United States.

Whereas, on September 11, 2001, acts of treacherous violence were committed against the United States and its citizens; and

Whereas, such acts render it both necessary and appropriate that the United States exercise its rights to self-defense and to protect United States citizens both at home and abroad; and

Whereas, in light of the threat to the national security and foreign policy of the United States posed by these grave acts of violence; and

Whereas, such acts continue to pose an unusual and extraordinary threat to the national security and foreign policy of the United States; and

Whereas, the President has authority under the Constitution to take action to deter and prevent acts of international terrorism against the United States:

Now, therefore, be it Resolved by the Senate and House of Representatives of the United States of America in Congress assembled,

§1. Short Title.

This joint resolution may be cited as the "Authorization for Use of Military Force."

§2. Authorization for Use of United States Armed Forces.

(a) In General.—That the President is authorized to use all necessary and appropriate force against those nations, organizations, or persons he determines planned, authorized, committed, or aided the terrorist attacks that occurred on September 11, 2001, or harbored such organizations or persons, in order to prevent any future acts of international terrorism against the United States by such nations, organizations or persons.

(b) War Powers Resolution Requirements.

(1) Specific statutory authorization.—Consistent with §8(a)(1) of the War Powers Resolution, the Congress declares that this section is intended to constitute specific statutory authorization within the meaning of §5(b) of the War Powers Resolution.

(2) Applicability of other requirements.—Nothing in this resolution supercedes [sic] any requirement of the War Powers Resolution.

the rather modest provisions in the Administration's anti-terrorist package pale by comparison. A long twilight struggle against terrorism that proves ineffective would chip away at the Constitution in ways Americans can scarcely imagine.[12]

———————●———————●———————●———————

Summary

Throughout the nation's history, it has been necessary to balance liberty and security. The September 11 attacks, the greatest threat since World War II, have forced us to place more emphasis on security. The Patriot Act expands the government's power, but to a much lesser extent than past wartime measures. Most of its provisions merely took existing legal principles and adapted them to modern technology. Despite warnings that the Patriot Act would lead to abuses, it has been narrowly focused on terrorists and their supporters. More importantly, the act has helped prevent another terrorist attack and the restrictions on liberty that would surely follow.

Antiterror Laws Are Ineffective and Dangerous

Critics allege that the Bush administration used the threat of another September 11–like attack to pressure Congress to pass the Patriot Act. They believe that lawmakers did not fully understand how it would curb civil liberties and expand government power. Legal experts and civil-liberties organizations have concluded that the act concentrates too much power in the executive branch, applies to crimes that have no relation to terrorism, and does nothing to address the government's mistakes that allowed September 11 to happen. More than three years have passed since the act became law. Some believe the time has come to take another look at it.

Antiterror Laws Are Too Broad

The fundamental problem with laws such as the Patriot Act is the word "terrorism" itself. International lawyer Richard

Whitbeck observes, "It is no accident that there is no agreed definition of 'terrorism,' since the word is so subjective as to be devoid of any inherent meaning. At the same time, the word is extremely dangerous, because people tend to believe that it does have meaning and to use and abuse the word by applying it to whatever they hate as a way of avoiding rational thought and discussion."[1]

> • **Is the word "terrorism" emotionally loaded? Do people even agree on what terrorism is?**

Section 802, which defines domestic terrorism, could lead to a repetition of the intelligence abuses of the 1960s, when government agents spied on antiwar activists and even civil rights leaders such as Dr. Martin Luther King, Jr. The Center for Constitutional Rights warns, "Rosa Parks, Martin Luther King, Jr., Fred Shuttlesworth, and the activists who stood beside them could have been charged with the crime of domestic terrorism for their acts of nonviolent civil disobedience. Their every move, their political activities, their personal relationships, their financial transactions, and their private records could have been monitored and recorded."[2]

> • **Is protest a sign of a healthy democracy? Is it a sign that people have lost faith in their leaders?**

The government justifies the Patriot Act as an antiterrorism law, but many of its provisions expand law-enforcement agencies' powers to fight ordinary crime. For example, §217 allows the government to monitor computers to catch hackers and §503 requires everyone convicted of a violent crime to provide a sample for the government's national DNA database. The government, by its own admission, has used it "to investigate suspected drug traffickers, white-collar criminals, blackmailers, child pornographers, money launderers, spies and even corrupt foreign leaders."[3] The Justice Department makes no apologies. A department spokesman said, "I think any reasonable person

THE LETTER OF THE LAW

The Offense of "Domestic Terrorism"

The Patriot Act was the first major federal antiterrorism law enacted since 1996. Several provisions of the act created new crimes, including that of "domestic terrorism." 18 U.S.C. Section 2331(5) provides:

The term "domestic terrorism" means activities that—

(A) involve acts dangerous to human life that are a violation of the criminal laws of the United States or of any State;

(B) appear to be intended—

 (i) to intimidate or coerce a civilian population;

 (ii) to influence the policy of a government by intimidation or coercion; or

 (iii) to affect the conduct of a government by mass destruction, assassination, or kidnapping; and

(C) occur primarily within the territorial jurisdiction of the United States.

Civil-liberties groups believe that opponents of the government could be prosecuted as domestic terrorists. The Center for Constitutional Rights believes that the definition of domestic terrorism is so vague that it may apply to acts of civil disobedience:

Civil disobedience typically seeks to influence government policy, and therefore may be construed as an attempt to coerce that change. Furthermore the portion of the definition stating that acts must be "dangerous to human life" is extremely broad: it does not distinguish between intentional acts and those that might cause inadvertent harm. Thus, a spontaneous demonstration that blocks the path of an ambulance might invite charges of domestic terrorism under the new law.[*]

The center warns that the law against domestic terrorism, whether enforced or not, will inhibit free speech because it creates the fear that political expression might be punished severely.

[*] Center for Constitutional Rights, The State of Civil Liberties, 2002. Available online at http://www.ccr-ny.org/v2/reports/docs/Civil_Liberities.pdf.

would agree that we have an obligation to do everything we can to protect the lives and liberties of Americans from attack, whether it's from terrorists or garden-variety criminals."[4] Some believe that the Bush administration used the September 11 attacks to pressure Congress into giving prosecutors legal powers that had long been on their "wish list."

It Is Too Easy to Abuse Antiterror Laws

One of the most dangerous aspects of the Patriot Act is that it gives the government wide-ranging authority to spy on Americans, even when investigating non-terrorism-related crimes. Section 213 of the act authorizes "sneak-and-peek" searches— the government can search first and notify the person searched afterward—in cases involving any federal crime. Section 216 expands the government's ability to monitor Internet usage, including e-mail addresses used and Websites visited, in "ongoing criminal investigations," whether terrorism related or not. The act has also increased the likelihood that innocent people will be spied on. Section 206 allows the FBI to monitor a computer in a public facility, such as a library, if it believes that by doing so it will find information relevant to a criminal investigation. The Internet activity of all users, not just suspects, now can be monitored.

- **Has fighting terrorism become a catchall excuse for greater government power?**

The Patriot Act also gives the government more access to individuals' personal data. One of its most controversial provisions, §215, allows the government to get a court order requiring the holder of "business records" to turn them over. The category of "business records" is extremely broad: It includes medical, credit card, and even library records.

The Patriot Act also makes it easier to carry out searches in secret: §215 imposes a "gag order" on those ordered to turn over business records, and §206 forbids a library or Internet café to

Price of security

There have been some
fundamental changes to
Americans' legal rights
since Sept. 11.

Freedom of Speech
Government may prosecute
librarians or keepers of any
other records if they tell anyone
that the government subpoenaed
information related to a terror investigation.

Right to legal representation
Government may monitor federal
prison conversations between
attorneys and clients, and
 deny lawyers to
Americans
accused of
crimes.

**Freedom from unreasonable
searches** Government may
search and seize Americans'
papers and effects
without probable
cause to assist
terror investigation.

Right to liberty
Americans may be jailed without
 being charged or
being able to
confront witnesses
against them.

**Right to a
speedy and
public trial**
Government
may jail Americans
indefinitely without a trial.

Freedom of Association
Government may monitor
religious and political
institutions without
suspecting
criminal activity
to assist terror
investigation.

Freedom of Information
Government has closed once-public
immigration hearings, has secretly
detained hundreds of people without
charges, and has
encouraged bureaucrats
to resist public records
requests.

SOURCE: Associated Press

AP

After September 11, the implementation of the Patriot Act changed Americans' legal rights and gave the U.S. government more access to individuals' personal data. This graphic gives a brief description of what changed.

warn computer users that they are being monitored. Innocent people have no way of knowing that investigators have been looking at their personal information. The American Civil

Liberties Union (ACLU), which has challenged the constitutionality of §215 in court, is concerned that it will discourage the exercise of the right to free speech: "There's a real possibility that setting the FBI loose on the American public will have a profound chilling effect on public discourse. If people think that their conversations and their e-mails or their reading habits are being monitored, people will inevitably feel less comfortable saying what they think, especially if what they think is not what the government wants them to think."[5]

Civil-liberties groups are concerned that several of the Patriot Act's provisions make it easier for the government to carry out "foreign intelligence" surveillance, which is governed by looser legal restrictions than searches for evidence of crime are. At the same time, the act makes it easier for the government to use foreign-intelligence surveillance to uncover criminals as well as spies and terrorists. In 1978, Congress required the government to show that foreign intelligence was "the purpose" of conducting surveillance. Section 218 of the Patriot Act lowered that standard: All the government now needs to show is that foreign intelligence is "a significant purpose" of the surveillance. In addition, applications for foreign intelligence surveillance are heard by a secret court, which by law is not supposed to second-guess the government. Since it was created, the court has reportedly turned down only one application.

> • **Are the government's claims of threats to national security exaggerated? Are they an excuse for keeping us in the dark?**

The Patriot Act also diminishes court supervision of searches in criminal cases. Section 220 authorizes nationwide search warrants, making it difficult for the court that issued the warrant to oversee investigators hundreds of miles away. One provision, §505, does away with the need for a court order when the FBI is investigating terrorism and has focused on a specific individual. All the FBI has to do is issue a "national security letter" ordering a holder of business records to turn them over.

The Patriot Act has not been the only reason for concern about abuse of power. After September 11, government agents arrested more than 1,000 people believed to have some connection to terrorism. Most were charged with immigration law violations, often minor ones. It was later discovered that some detainees were held for months, denied access to a lawyer, or mistreated while in custody. Human-rights groups sued the government for details about the roundup, but a federal appeals court agreed with the government that releasing the information—even the names of those detained—would endanger national security. Judge David Tatel, who dissented, suggested that the government might have covered up its violations of the law: "History . . . is full of examples of situations in which just these sorts of allegations led to the discovery of serious government wrongdoing—from Teapot Dome in the 1920s to the FBI's COINTELPRO counterintelligence program in the 1960s to Watergate in the 1970s."[6]

The Justice Department and other agencies have argued repeatedly that national security requires them to operate in secret. Professor Ronald Dworkin replies, "This is an argument made by every police state, and it may be the most self-serving and indefensible claim the Bush administration has made so far."[7]

Laws Alone Will Not Prevent Terrorist Attacks

The Patriot Act makes it easier for law-enforcement agencies to collect information they think is relevant to terrorist activity. Critics insist that the government is missing the point. They question whether more information, by itself, will prevent another attack. In fact, the added information might make it more difficult to find terrorists. For example, the government's "Visas Condor" program screened more than 100,000 Arab and Muslim men who applied for American visas. The program found no terrorists and created a backlash that hurt America's tourism industry. Many observers insist that the biggest problem is not a lack of information but rather a lack of trained personnel—especially those who read and speak Arabic—to analyze it.

It is also becoming clear that a major reason for the September 11 attacks was the government's failure to act on the information it already had. A study by the Merkel Family Foundation found that two of the hijackers' names were on a government list of suspected terrorists and that further data checks—looking for who lived at the same address, used the same phone number, or had the same frequent-flyer number as the two suspects—might have identified other members of the hijacking plot. Some have also suggested that, before asking for new laws, the authorities should do a better job of enforcing those already on the books. Critics claim that immigration authorities were especially lax: They allowed foreign visitors to overstay their visas and did not pressure colleges to comply with laws requiring them to turn over information about foreign students.

It Is Impossible to Eliminate the Risk of Terror

Long before the September 11 attacks, there was widespread fear of terrorism. In 1986, we rated it our number-one concern, even though lightning killed four times as many Americans as terrorists did that year. Even in the tragic year of 2001, when terrorists killed nearly 3,000 people on September 11, drunk drivers claimed more lives than terrorists: According to the Department of Transportation, 17,448 people died that year in alcohol-related crashes.[8] Critics accuse political leaders of using the threat of more attacks to frighten the public into giving up their freedom. As national security specialist David Aaron points out, the risk of terrorism can never be reduced to zero: "We may be able to disrupt the terrorists' operations, keep them on the run, neutralize their key leaders, undermine the governments that provide sanctuary—in short, we should be able to control

POLL

Terror vs. freedom

Americans are concerned that efforts to fight terrorism could eventually encroach on their personal freedom.

1. Do you have a favorable or unfavorable opinion of Attorney General John Ashcroft?

39%	Favorable
20%	Unfavorable
41%	Don't know

2. How concerned are you that new measures to fight terrorism in this country could restrict our individual freedom?

34%	Very
32%	Somewhat
19%	Not very
14%	Not at all
1%	Don't know

3. Do you think that in efforts against terrorism, the United States has or has not violated the legal rights and individual freedom of people living in the United States?

31%	Yes
58%	No
11%	Don't know

4. In order to curb terrorism in this country, do you think it will be necessary for the average person to give up some individual freedom or not?

51%	Yes
43%	No
6%	Don't know

5. Do you think the Bush administration has gone too far or not far enough in using new laws that give the government more power to fight terrorism?

24%	Too far
49%	About right
18%	Not far enough
9%	Don't know

About this poll: The poll of 1,008 adults was taken Sept. 4-8 by ICR/International Communications Research of Media, Pa. and has a margin of error of plus or minus 3 percentage points.

AP

An Associated Press poll in 2003 investigated Americans' feelings about measures taken by the U.S. government to fight terrorism. This chart shows, in percentages, how the 1,008 adults polled responded to each question.

and minimize the level of Islamic terrorism—but it seems unlikely that it can be eliminated entirely." [9]

Furthermore, surrendering our freedoms means abandoning what defines us as Americans in the first place. Russ Feingold, the only senator to vote against the Patriot Act, explains, "The Founders who wrote our Constitution and Bill of Rights exercised that vigilance even though they had recently fought and won the Revolutionary War. They did not live in comfortable and easy times of hypothetical enemies. They wrote a Constitution of limited powers and an explicit Bill of Rights to protect liberty in times of war, as well as in times of peace." [10]

Antiterror Laws Encourage Discrimination

In past conflicts, members of minority groups suffered from abuse of government power: German Americans were targeted during World War I, Japanese Americans during World War II. In the war on terror, the scapegoats are Arabs and Muslims, who were viewed with suspicion even before September 11. During the debate over the Patriot Act, Senator Feingold warned that this would happen: "Who do we think that is most likely to bear the brunt of the abuse? It won't be immigrants from Ireland. It won't be immigrants from El Salvador or Nicaragua. It won't even be immigrants from Haiti or Africa. It will be immigrants from Arab, Muslim and South Asian countries." [11]

After the September 11 attacks, federal agents interviewed thousands of Arab and Muslim men, who felt they had no choice but to cooperate, and jailed and deported many of them for immigration offenses once considered "technical." Georgetown University law professor David Cole was highly critical of the government's heavy-handed tactics: "What the government has done, again, is to take its tremendously broad power over foreign nationals and use it as a pretext to round up specific groups—in this case Arabs and Muslims. . . . The result, to date, is virtually no new terrorists identified, no further participants in 9/11 identified, and a deeply alienated community." [12]

- **Have Arabs and Muslims been persecuted by Americans or the U.S. government since September 11?**

The post–September 11 crackdown, which some call a classic case of racial profiling, was not limited to immigrants. Arab Americans reported a sharp increase in incidents of discrimination and harassment, especially multiple searches and

FROM THE BENCH

Personal Justice Denied: The Japanese Internment Cases

In the months after Pearl Harbor, the Japanese military swept across the western Pacific, leading to fears that the West Coast might be attacked. The military was also concerned that some of the more than 100,000 ethnic Japanese living on the West Coast would side with the enemy.

In February 1942, President Roosevelt issued an executive order authorizing military commanders to take steps they considered necessary to prevent espionage and sabotage. Shortly afterward, Congress made disobedience of military restrictions a misdemeanor, thus allowing civilian courts to sentence violators. Acting under the president's order, military authorities imposed a nighttime curfew on ethnic Japanese living in military zones and later ordered them to report to relocation centers, the first step in the process of interning them in camps away from the West Coast. Court challenges to those restrictions led to two of the most controversial decisions in Supreme Court history.

The first case involved Kiyoshi Hirabayashi, a college student living in Seattle. Hirabayashi appealed his conviction for violating the curfew and failing to report to a relocation center. He argued that the military orders discriminated against him on account of his ethnicity. The case went up to the Supreme Court, which, in Hirabayashi v. United States, 320 U.S. 81 (1943), unanimously upheld his conviction.

The Court's opinion, written by Chief Justice Harlan Stone, rested on the principle that courts deferred to the other branches of government in matters related to war. The chief justice found that the military had reason to believe ethnic Japanese would sabotage the war effort and that a curfew was an appropriate means of preventing it. Although racial discrimination was usually prohibited, it was permissible if "residents having different ethnic affiliations identification checks at airports, a phenomenon they called "flying while brown." Former Vice President Al Gore called the government's actions a "cheap and cruel publicity stunt": "More than 99% of the mostly Arab-background men who were rounded up had merely overstayed their visas or committed some other minor offense. . . . But they were used as extras in the Administration's effort to give the impression that they had

with an invading enemy may be a greater source of danger than those of a different ancestry."

The Hirabayashi Court put off ruling on the constitutionality of the forced relocation of ethnic Japanese. Because Hirabayashi had been sentenced to concurrent jail terms for violating two different orders, the Court only needed to find one of them—the curfew order—constitutional, saving the issue of whether the government could force the Japanese into camps for another day.

That day came when the Court decided Korematsu v. United States, 323 U.S. 214 (1944). Toyosaburo Korematsu appealed his conviction for refusing to leave San Leandro, California, a military area from which ethnic Japanese were excluded. Korematsu's appeal went to the Supreme Court, which, by a 6–3 vote, upheld his conviction.

Justice Hugo Black's majority opinion focused on Korematsu's exclusion: "Regardless of the true nature of the assembly and relocation centers—and we deem it unjustifiable to call them concentration camps with all the ugly connotations that term implies—we are dealing specifically with nothing but an exclusion order."

He concluded that, although restrictions aimed at a single racial group deserved "the most rigid scrutiny," the wartime exclusion of ethnic Japanese from a threatened area had "a definite and close relationship to the prevention of espionage and sabotage." Although the United States was now winning the war, Justice Black refused to second-guess the military's determination that there were disloyal Japanese whose exclusion was necessary.

The three dissenting justices condemned the unequal treatment of ethnic Japanese. Justice Owen Roberts also accused the majority of avoiding the real issue: forcing people into camps solely because of their ancestry and without evidence that they were disloyal. Justice Frank Murphy questioned the military's contention that their relocation was necessary to prevent sabotage. Justice Robert Jackson argued that the Court had made a mistake by deciding the constitutionality of the president's military orders in the first place. He believed that it would have been wiser to let the voters, not the courts, serve as the ultimate check on the president's use of his war powers.

The same day it decided Korematsu, the Court also decided Ex Parte Endo, 323 U.S. 283 (1944), which concluded that the interment of at least some Japanese Americans was unconstitutional. Mitsuye Endo, a Japanese American who had been transported to a camp in Utah, filed a habeas corpus petition. The Court unanimously sided with Endo, finding that the government had conceded her loyalty yet delayed her release because local officials feared an uncontrolled migration of ethnic Japanese into their communities. Speaking for a unanimous Court, Justice William Douglas wrote, "A citizen who is concededly loyal presents no problem of espionage or sabotage. Loyalty is a matter of the heart and mind not of race, creed, or color. He who is loyal is by definition not a spy or a saboteur."

Reading Korematsu and Endo together, the Court concluded that a Japanese American had no right to defy the military's relocation order but, once interned in a camp, could file a habeas corpus petition alleging that he or she was a loyal citizen and therefore detained unlawfully. Many believe that this awkward result supports the notion that the Court should have avoided ruling on the constitutionality of the president's military orders. The Court's current chief justice, William Rehnquist, suggests, "If, in fact, courts are more prone to uphold wartime claims of civil liberties after the war is over, may it not actually be desirable to avoid decision on such claims during the war?"*

In any event, historians consider the Japanese internment one of the more shameful episodes in American legal history. In 1983, a federal commission issued a report called Personal Justice Denied, which concluded that the internment was not justified by military necessity and that the Supreme Court decisions upholding it were "overruled in the court of history." The following year, U.S. District Judge Marilyn Patel issued an order vacating Korematsu's conviction. In doing so, she concluded that the claim of military necessity for President Roosevelt's order was based on "unsubstantiated facts, distortions and representations of at least one military commander, whose views were seriously infected by racism."**

* Rehnquist, William. All Laws But One: Civil Liberties in Wartime. New York: Alfred A. Knopf, 1998, p. 222.

** Commission on Wartime Relocation and Internment of Civilians. Personal Justice Denied. Washington, D.C.: Government Printing Office, 1982.

caught a large number of bad guys."[13] Others contended that the government did more harm than good, making Arabs and Muslims suspicious of the government when their cooperation was most needed.

* * *

Summary

The war on terror has resulted in broader power for law-enforcement agencies and a diminished role for courts in guarding against abuse of power. Laws aimed at terrorism have been used to pursue ordinary criminals, target members of minority groups, and spy on innocent citizens. In addition, the government is operating more secretly, making it harder to expose abuses of power. Critics believe that the government's new powers erode civil liberties but do little to address the intelligence failures that led to the September 11 attacks.

The Future of the War Against Terror

After the September 11 attacks, President Bush described the problem we face: "In a globalized world, events beyond America's borders have a greater impact inside them. . . . The characteristics we most cherish—our freedom, our cities, our systems of movement, and modern life—are vulnerable to terrorism." [1]

The president described terrorism as "a new condition of life" and warned that we will be vulnerable even after those responsible for September 11 are brought to justice. Since then, there has been heated debate over the best way to combat terrorism both at home and abroad.

Legal and Political Issues

The government's antiterror strategy has led to disagreements among political leaders and legal experts and to lawsuits challenging the government's new powers. The four legal and political issues likely to be debated include these:

1. **The Future of the Patriot Act:** Did the Patriot Act strike the right balance between liberty and security? In 2003, several senators introduced the Security and Freedom Ensured (SAFE) Act,[2] which would place limits on business-records searches, "sneak-and-peek" searches, and roving wiretaps. Senator Richard Durbin, a cosponsor, commented, "[I]n some cases the [Patriot Act] goes too far, and we should amend those provisions to reflect every American citizen's right to be both safe and free.[3]

   President Bush and his supporters, however, believe that the act did not provide law-enforcement agencies with all the legal tools they need. He urged Congress to expand the FBI's authority to obtain information without a court order, allow courts to deny bail to accused terrorists, and make additional terror-related crimes punishable by death.

   Those provisions are part of the proposed Domestic Security Enhancement Act, or "Patriot II," which was drafted by the Justice Department and leaked to the public. Patriot II would expand the scope of government surveillance and increase the amount of secrecy surrounding antiterrorism efforts. Patriot II was never submitted to Congress, but some fear that it will be if terrorists strike again. Others are afraid that Patriot II will be passed in piecemeal fashion. A provision in an intelligence spending bill passed in 2003 broadened the definition of "financial institution."[4] Now the FBI is able to demand records from travel agencies, pawn shops, and other businesses.

   Another battle is likely to involve the Patriot Act's "sunset" provision, under which some of its most controversial provisions will expire automatically at the end of 2005. In his 2004 State of the Union Address, President Bush told Congress, "The terrorist threat will not expire on that schedule. Our law enforcement needs this vital legislation to protect our citizens. You need to renew the Patriot Act."[5]

2. **Collection and Use of Personal Information:** "Data mining," the analysis of large amounts of personal information stored in public computers, has been

National Security Versus the Public's Right to Know

Human-rights groups and the news media went to court to challenge the secrecy surrounding the government's actions after the September 11 attacks. The government insists that national security requires it to maintain secrecy: If terrorists learn about enforcement activity, even minor details, they would learn how the government was fighting them and change their tactics accordingly. So far, the courts have been receptive to the government's argument. Important decisions relating to secrecy include these:

- **Use of secret evidence:** In Global Relief Foundation v. O'Neill, 315 F.3d 748 (7th Cir. 2002), a federal appeals court upheld an order freezing the assets of a charity designated as a terrorist organization by the treasury secretary, even though the lower court refused to disclose some of the government's evidence in support of the freeze order. The court stated, "The Constitution would indeed be a suicide pact . . . if the only way to curtail enemies' access to assets were to reveal information that might cost lives." In November 2003, the Supreme Court decided not to review the appeals court's decision.

- **Nondisclosure of arrests and detentions:** In Center for National Security Studies v. Department of Justice, 331 F.3d 918 (D.C. Cir. 2003), a federal appeals court upheld the government's refusal to release information about the post-September 11 arrests of hundreds of people. It concluded that the information was not disclosable under the Freedom of Information Act because the government had shown that making it available could provide in the news lately. The purpose of data mining is to discover hidden patterns or "profiles." Businesses mine data to find customers who respond to advertising or who buy certain products. Data mining has also been used to detect fraud. The most controversial data-mining proposal, the Defense Department's "Total Information Awareness" program, would have analyzed educational, medical, credit, and other records to uncover possible terrorist activity. TIA was so heavily criticized that Congress cut off funding for

terrorists with a "road map" of its investigations. In January 2004, the Supreme Court decided not to review the appeals court's decision.

- **Closed immigration hearings:** Two federal appeals courts came to opposite conclusions on a Justice Department order closing all immigration hearings involving persons suspected of having ties to terrorist groups. In Detroit Free Press, et al. v. Ashcroft, 303 F.3d 681 (6th Cir. 2002), the Sixth Circuit concluded that, although national security was a "compelling reason" for closing hearings, the government had not shown why it was necessary to close all hearings rather than decide on a case-by-case basis. In North Jersey Media Group, et al. v. Ashcroft, 308 F.3d 198 (3rd Cir. 2002), however, the Third Circuit found the blanket closure of hearings constitutional. It concluded that immigration hearings did not have a history of openness, and, even if they did, the national-security risks outweighed the benefits of open hearings.

- **Secret court proceedings:** One of the most unusual post-September 11 cases is M.K.B. v. Warden, No. 03-6747. It began with Mohammed Kamel Bellahouel's detention on immigration charges. While in custody, he filed a habeas corpus petition. The courts not only excluded the public from his hearings, but also sealed the entire record of the case (Bellahouel's name was disclosed when the appeals court mistakenly posted it on a public docket). Although Bellahouel was released after five months, his lawsuit remains alive because he still might be deported. In February 2004, the Supreme Court denied Bellahouel's appeal. The Court also refused to allow a coalition of news-media and public-interest groups to join the case and challenge the security imposed by the government and the lower courts.

it. The Defense Department has proposed a modified version of TIA and is believed to be developing other surveillance programs. More recently, the government proposed CAPPS II, which would have checked government and commercial databases to identify

THE LETTER OF THE LAW

Major Provisions of "Patriot II"

In early 2003, a Justice Department draft of the proposed "Domestic Security Enhancement Act," or "Patriot II," was leaked to the Center for Public Integrity, an advocacy group in Washington.* Major provisions of the Act include these:

§101. Expands the definition of "foreign power," for purposes of foreign intelligence surveillance, to include "lone wolf" terrorists and "sleeper cells."

§105. Gives federal authorities wider powers to share foreign-intelligence information.

§124. Authorizes surveillance of all functions of a multifunction device such as a BlackBerry.

§125. Expands the list of alleged offenses for which judges may issue nationwide search warrants.

§128. Widens the Justice Department's power to issue "administrative subpoenas," which do not require a court order, for information relating to a terrorism investigation. A person may not disclose the fact that he was subpoenaed.

§129(c). Gives terrorism and espionage investigators more authority to share information with other federal agencies.

§201. Amends the Freedom of Information Act to allow the government to withhold information about individuals detained in terrorism investigations.

§302. Authorizes the FBI to collect DNA samples from people suspected of terrorism as well as those convicted of terror-related crimes.

§311. Allows federal agencies to share information with state and local law-enforcement agencies.

§312. Voids most court orders from the 1970s and 1980s that restrict the power of police departments to gather information about suspected terrorists.

airline passengers who might pose a security risk. Critics argued that CAPPS II was expensive, threatened privacy, and would not catch terrorists. In July 2004, the Department of Homeland Security canceled the program.

§313. Shields businesses from civil liability for having disclosed personal information to a federal agency investigating terrorism.

§401. Creates a new offense of perpetrating a terrorism hoax.

§404. Imposes an additional prison term of at least five years for use of computer encryption to hide evidence that a person had committed a federal felony.

§405. Denies bail to most accused terrorists.

§408. Allows for longer periods of postrelease supervision of convicted terrorists who have served their prison terms.

§410. Eliminates the statute of limitations for terror-related crimes.

§411. Expands the list of terrorism offenses punishable by death.

§421. Increases civil fines for financing terrorist organizations.

§424. Denies federal benefits, such as student loans and commercial licenses, to convicted terrorists.

§501. Allows the government to strip an American of citizenship for serving in a hostile army or terrorist organization.

§503. Allows the Justice Department to bar from the country a person who poses a threat to national security or who was convicted of a serious crime elsewhere.

§504. Makes it easier to deport noncitizens, including green card holders, who have committed a crime in the United States.

* Center for Public Integrity. Available online at http://www.publicintegrity.org/docs/PatriotAct/story_01_020703_doc_1.pdf.

3. **National Identity Cards:** The September 11 attacks revived discussion of whether Americans should carry national identity cards. The idea is strongly opposed by many Americans and by the Bush administration. Supporters believe that the card would help prevent terrorism by making it harder to establish a false identity and would also reduce problems such as identity theft and illegal gun sales. Opponents argue that asking citizens for "your papers, please," is the hallmark of a police state, not a free country such as the United States. They also contend that the cards will lead to racial profiling and the collection of personal data and will not stop sophisticated terrorists from creating false identities.

4. **Profiling:** The September 11 attacks also focused attention on *profiling*, or concentrating law-enforcement efforts on those who meet a set of criteria associated with certain crimes. Profiling came under attack when it was revealed that African Americans were more likely to be stopped by the police, especially while driving. Advocates believe that profiling is not only smart police work but needed to fight terrorist acts, especially airline hijacking. Because most al Qaeda members are young men of Middle Eastern origin, supporters believe that passengers meeting that description should receive close scrutiny. They claim that this is not done for reasons of political correctness, and, as a result, passengers must put up with random checks that many consider a waste of time. On the other hand, opponents believe that profiling does not work because terrorists will outsmart profilers. According to former Congressman Bob Barr, "As the CIA itself noted in a unclassified study reportedly conducted in 2001, terrorists typically take great pains to avoid being profiled: they don't want

to get caught, and in fact it is essentially impossible to profile terrorists."[6]

> • Do you think the police are more likely to stop members of minority groups? Young people? Those who look different?

A Clash of Civilizations?

In 1993, Samuel Huntington, who now chairs Howard University's Academy of International and Area Studies, predicted, "The great divisions among humankind and the dominating source of conflict will be cultural. . . . The clash of civilizations will dominate global politics. The fault lines between civilizations will be the battle lines of the future."[7] Huntington believes that the clash between the Western and Islamic worlds has been going on for more than 1,000 years and that it has intensified since the end of the Cold War, in Chechnya and Bosnia, for example.

> • Does American culture offend people in the Middle East? What would you tell young Arabs and Muslims about America?

Huntington's theory is controversial. Some believe that it justifies the kind of discrimination that took place after September 11 and creates the perception that Westerners and Muslims can never live in peace (Huntington believes that coexistence is possible but will be difficult). Others insist that a cultural clash is unavoidable. They point to the spread of "political Islam," a radical ideology that views the United States as an "evil empire" and opposes Western ideas such as democracy and capitalism. Political Islam is attracting young Muslims, even those who are not strongly religious, because they see the fight against terror as a war against them. Some Americans believe that the Islamic world is already at war with us. One newspaper editorial bluntly stated:

> America is hated and feared by the clerical and political classes
> —the only ones that matter—from North Africa to Southeast Asia.

This hatred is so widespread and powerful that it unites ancient rivals. Sunnis and Shiites, Persians and Arabs, Baathists and royalists, tribal leaders and urban intellectuals, theologians and supposedly secular military officers—all gather under the banner of *jihad*.[8]

Other Terrorist Threats

Americans associate terrorism with the Middle East. Experts believe that radical Muslims will not be the only terrorists of the future, however. These experts offer a variety of predictions about the changing face of terrorism. The Hart-Rudman report on national security warns that civil wars will breed new terrorist movements and weaken some governments to the point that they can no longer control terrorist organizations. Parts of Southeast Asia, South America, and especially Africa could be the home of future terrorists. Meanwhile, experts warn of a rising danger from homegrown terrorists like the Unabomber. Walter Laqueur, Co-Chair of the Center for Strategic and International Studies, thinks that future terrorists are more likely to be "lone wolves" with weapons of mass destruction, like the "mad scientists" in old science-fiction movies.

Experts offer a variety of ideas about future terrorists' weapons of choice. The number-one concern is weapons of mass destruction (WMDs). The Hart-Rudman Commission believes that if a WMD attack comes, it will most likely be biological. Professor Laqueur warns of the destructive potential of "cyber-warfare": "If the new terrorism directs its energies toward information warfare, its destructive power will be exponentially greater than any it wielded in the past—greater even than it would be with biological and chemical weapons."[9]

Some expect a methodical series of suicide bombings in a city such as New York or attacks by terrorist cells with military training and weapons. These relatively low-intensity attacks would make Americans think twice about going to public gatherings—even going to church or sending their children to school—and seriously damage the economy.

> • **Has America "turned the corner" in the fight against terrorism? Is another September 11 inevitable?**

Battling for Hearts and Minds

Although the American-led military campaign in Afghanistan has seriously damaged al Qaeda, experts warn that force alone will not eliminate the terrorist threat. The British, who have faced terrorists around the world, learned the hard way that fighting terrorism is a struggle for "hearts and minds" and that the misuse of force—such as firing on Irish Republican Army (IRA) demonstrators on "Bloody Sunday" in 1972—provides terrorists with a propaganda victory. Some question whether the West is doing enough to win hearts and minds in the Middle East and warn that we are creating a generation of extremists who see terrorism as the only way to fight back. A memo by Defense Secretary Donald Rumsfeld suggested that we could lose the fight against terrorism: "Are we capturing, killing or deterring and dissuading more terrorists every day than the *madrassas* [Islamic religious schools] and the radical clerics are recruiting, training and deploying against us? The cost-benefit ratio is against us! Our cost is billions against the terrorists' costs of millions." [10]

Critics also maintain that we are doing too little to address the root causes of terrorism. They urge the United States to stop supporting corrupt dictatorships, help countries build economies based on brain power rather than on oil, and pursue a more evenhanded peace policy in the Middle East.

When Will the War on Terror End?

After the September 11 attacks, President Bush told Congress, "Our war on terror begins with al Qaeda, but it does not end there. It will not end until every terrorist group of global reach has been found, stopped and defeated." [11] Most Americans expect a long conflict. According to an October 2003 CBS News poll, 24 percent of Americans believe that the war on terror will last longer than 10 years, and another 34 percent believe it will last "a long time" or "forever."

> • **Will we know when the war on terror is over? Is it possible to know?**

For that reason, some observers are uncomfortable with calling the fight against terror a "war." Professor Ronald Dworkin argues, "We fight conventional wars against nations that have boundaries, and leaders with whom we can negotiate truces and surrenders, not against loose organizations whose hierarchies are secret and indistinct and whose officers and soldiers do not wear uniforms. We can conquer Kabul and Baghdad, but there is no place called Terror where the terrorists live."[12] Others believe that the war analogy led the public to expect quick and spectacular results, when in fact the biggest successes against terrorism will be those the public never sees on the nightly news.

Still, America's immediate problem is al Qaeda and terrorist groups affiliated with and trained by it. Terrorism experts Daniel Benjamin and Steven Simon lay out a strategy to defeat it: "For the next few years, the objective . . . will be to contain the threat, much as the United States contained Soviet power throughout the cold war. The adversary must be prevented from doing his worst, while the United States and its allies wear down his capabilities and undermine the support he derives from coreligionists."[13] They also believe we have to "convince Muslim populations that they can prosper without either destroying the West or abandoning their traditions to the onslaught of Western culture."[14]

However the fight against terrorism it is labeled, the question remains, how and when will it end? Some compare it to the Vietnam War, which was as much a struggle for hearts and minds as for supremacy on the battlefield. Others liken it to the Thirty Years' War (1618–1648), a bloody conflict between Catholic and Protestant rulers that did not end until millions of

Europeans were dead and the warring sides were too exhausted to fight. Still others think the fight against terror will resemble the Cold War, a "long twilight struggle" that finally ended with the collapse of Communism. Experts have differing opinions on how the war on terror should be fought, but they do agree on one thing: It will be a difficult and drawn-out conflict.

- **Can the Western world and the Islamic world live together in peace?**

Summary

The war on terror has led to debate about whether additional government powers are needed at home and about the best way to deal with terrorists overseas. Domestic issues include the future of the Patriot Act—opinion about it remains sharply divided—and whether additional measures such as stepped-up surveillance are needed to prevent another attack. Foreign policy issues include whether the fight against terror can be won by force alone, whether we are winning the hearts and minds of Arabs and Muslims, and how to address the root causes of terrorism. Americans are debating how best to defeat al Qaeda and prevent attacks by terrorists of the future.

Introduction

1 Daniel Benjamin and Steven Simon, *The Age of Sacred Terror*, New York, NY: Random House, 2002, pp. 350–351.

2 United States Commission on National Security/21st Century, *Seeking a National Strategy: A Concert for Preserving Security and Promoting Freedom*. Washington, D.C.: United States Commission on National Security/21st Century, 2000, p. 5. Available online at *http://www.nssg.gov/PhaseII.pdf*.

3 George W. Bush, Address to Joint Session of Congress, September 20, 2001. Available online at *http://whitehouse.gov/news/releases/2001/09/print/20010920-8.html*.

4 Ibid.

5 George W. Bush, Graduation Speech, United States Military Academy, June 1, 2002. Available online at *http://www.whitehouse.gov/news/releases/2002/06/print/20020601-3.html*.

6 Office of the President of the United States, *The National Security Strategy of the United States of America*. Washington, D.C.: Office of the President of the United States, 2002, p. 6. Available online at *http://www.whitehouse.gov/nsc/nss.pdf*.

Point: The United States Must Act Decisively to Defend Itself

1 George W. Bush, State of the Union Address, January 29, 2002. Available online at *http://www.whitehouse.gov/news/releases/2002/01/print/20020129-11.html*.

2 George W. Bush, Remarks on Iraq, Cincinnati, Ohio, October 7, 2002. Available online at *http://www.whitehouse.gov/news/releases/2002/10/print/20021007-8.html*.

3 John F. Kennedy, Radio and Television Report to the American People on the Soviet Arms Buildup in Cuba, October 22, 1962. Available online at *http://www.jfklibrary.org/j102262.htm*.

4 Gary Schmitt, Memorandum to Opinion Leaders: Richard Perle on Iraq. Washington, D.C.: Project for the New American Century, 2003. Available online at *http://www.newamericancentury.org/iraq-20030224.htm*.

5 George W. Bush, Remarks at Whitehall Palace, London, England, November 19, 2003. Available online at *http://www.whitehouse.gov/news/releases/2003/11/print/20031119-1.html*.

6 Max Boot, *The Savage Wars of Peace: Small Wars and the Rise of American Power*. New York, NY: Basic Books, 2002, p. 349.

7 Schmitt, Memorandum to Opinion Leaders. Available online at *http://www.newamericancentury.org/iraq-20030224.htm*.

8 Carla Anne Robbins, "Operation Bypass: Why the U.S. Gave the U.N. No Role in Plan to Halt Arms Ships," *The Wall Street Journal*, October 21, 2003.

9 David B. Rivkin, Jr., and Lee A. Casey, "The Rocky Shoals of International Law," *The National Interest* 62, Winter 2000/2001, p. 35.

10 Reuel Marc Gerecht, "A Necessary War: Unless Saddam Hussein is Removed, The War on Terror Will Fail," *The Weekly Standard*, October 21, 2002, p. 6. Available online at *http://www.weeklystandard.com/Content/Public/Articles/000/000/001/768lyuyh.asp*.

Counterpoint: Unilateralism and Preemptive War Do More Harm Than Good

1 United Nations Security Council Resolution No. 1378 (November 14, 2001).

2 Jeffrey Record, *Bounding the Global War on Terrorism*. Carlisle, PA: U.S. Army War College, 2003, p. 49 (footnote 51). Available online at *http://www.carlisle.army.mil/ssi/pubs/2003/bounding/bounding.pdf*.

3 Association of the Bar of New York City, Committee on International Security Affairs, *The Legality and Constitutionality of the President's Authority to Initiate an*

Invasion of Iraq. Draft. New York: Association of the Bar of New York City, 2002, p.12. Available online at *http://www .abcny.org/pdf/report/Iraq2.pdf.*

4 Rivkin and Casey, "The Rocky Shoals of International Law," p. 35.

5 Michael Ignatieff, "Why Are We in Iraq? (And Liberia? And Afghanistan?)," *New York Times Magazine*, September 7, 2003, p. 38

6 Richard A. Falk, "The Aftermath of 9/11 and the Search for Limits: In Defense of Just War Thinking." In Charles W. Kegley, Jr., ed., *The New Global Terrorism: Characteristics, Causes, Controls.* Upper Saddle River, NJ: Prentice-Hall, 2003, p. 218.

7 Bill Christison, "Former Senior CIA Officer: Why the 'War on Terror' Won't Work." CounterPunch.org, March 4, 2002. Available online at *http://www .counterpunch.org/christison1.html.*

8 Michael Howard, "What's in a Name? How to Fight Terrorism," 81 Foreign Aff. 8 (2002).

9 Michael Ignatieff, "Why America Must Know Its Limits," *Financial Times*, December 24, 2003.

10 Record, p. 43. Available online at *http://www.carlisle.army.mil/ssi/ pdffiles/00200.pdf.*

11 Ignatieff, "Why America Must Know Its Limits."

12 Ibid.

Point: Military Justice Is an Appropriate Way to Deal With Terrorists

1 *Hirabayashi* v. *United States*, 320 U.S. 81, 93 (1943).

2 *Hamdi* v. *Rumsfeld*, 316 F.3d 450, 466 (4th Cir. 2003).

3 David B. Rivkin, Jr. and Lee A. Casey, "Guantanamo on Trial: The Red Cross Makes a Big Mistake in Siding With Detained Terrorists," *The Wall Street Journal*, November 19, 2003.

4 Bradford A. Berenson, "Earth to Second Circuit: We're At War," *The Wall Street Journal*, December 29, 2003.

5 Laurie Mylroie, *The War Against America: Saddam Hussein and the World Trade Center Attacks.* New York: Harper-Collins Publishers, 2001, p. 116.

6 Mylroie, p. 247.

7 Berenson, "Earth to Second Circuit."

8 Kenneth Anderson, "What to Do with Bin Laden and Al Qaeda Terrorists?: A Qualified Defense of Military Commissions and United States Policy on Detainees at Guantanamo Bay Naval Base." 25 Harv. J.L. & Pub. Pol'y. 593 (2002).

9 Robert H. Bork, "Civil Liberties After 9/11." 116 Commentary 29 (2003).

Counterpoint: The War on Terror Violates Human Rights

1 Anne-Marie Slaughter, "Beware the Trumpets of War: A Response to Kenneth Anderson." 25 Harv. J.L. & Pub. Pol'y. 965 (2002).

2 Howard, "What's in a Name?," p. 8.

3 Diane F. Orentlicher and Robert K. Goldman, "When Justice Goes to War: Prosecuting Terrorists Before Military Commissions." 25 Harv. J.L. & Pub. Pol'y. 653 (2002).

4 Al Gore, "Freedom and Security." Address to MoveOn.org, November 9, 2003. Available online at *http://www .moveon.org/gore/speech2.html.*

5 American Bar Association Task Force on Terrorism and the Law, *Report and Recommendation on Military Commissions.* Chicago: American Bar Association, 2002, p. 6. Available online at *http://www.abanet.org/poladv/letters/ exec/militarycomm_report.pdf.*

6 Orentlicher and Goldman, p. 653.

7 Center for Constitutional Rights, *The State of Civil Liberties: One Year Later. Erosion of Civil Liberties in the Post-9/11 Era.* New York: Center for Constitutional Rights, p. 16. Available online at *http://www.ccr-ny.org/v2/reports/docs/ Civil_Liberties.pdf.*

8 John V. Whitbeck, "'Terrorism': The Word Itself is Dangerous." *Washington Report on Middle East Affairs* 21, March 2002, p. 52.

9 Gore, "Freedom and Security." Available online at *http://www.moveon.org/gore/speech2.html.*

10 Edwin Dobb, "Should John Walker Lindh Go Free?" *Harper's Magazine,* May 2002, p. 31.

11 Association of the Bar of the City of New York, Inter Arma Silent Leges? *In Time of Armed Conflict,* Should *the Laws Be Silent?* New York: Association of the Bar of the City of New York, p. 41. Available online at *http://www.abcny.org/pdf/should_the_laws.pdf.*

12 Ibid., p. 40.

Point: New Laws Are Needed to Fight Terrorism

1 U.S. Department of Justice. Undated. *USA PATRIOT Act Overview.* Washington, D.C.: U.S. Department of Justice, p 1. Available online at *http://www.lifeandliberty.gov/patriot_overview_pversion.pdf.*

2 Ibid.

3 Stewart Baker, "Wall Nuts: The Wall Between Intelligence and Law Enforcement is Killing Us," Slate.com, December 31, 2003. Available online at *http://slate.msn.com/id/2093344.*

4 Ibid.

5 Ibid.

6 William H. Rehnquist, *All Laws But One: Civil Liberties in Wartime.* New York: Alfred A. Knopf, pp. 224–225.

7 American Library Association, Resolution on the USA Patriot Act and Related Measures That Infringe on the Rights of Library Users. Chicago: American Library Association, 2003. Available online at *http://www.ala.org/Template.cfm?Section=ifresolutions&Template=/ContentManagement/ContentDisplay.cfm&ContentID=11891.*

8 §215, Public Law 107-56, The USA-PATRIOT Act.

9 John Ashcroft, Testimony Before the House Judiciary Committee, July 5, 2003. Available online at *http://www.lifeandliberty.gov/subs/speeches/a_ashcroft_060503.htm.*

10 Ibid.

11 Kim R. Holmes and Edwin Meese, III, *The Administration's Anti-Terrorism Package: Balancing Security and Liberty.* Heritage Foundation Backgrounder No. 1484. Washington D.C.: Heritage Foundation, 2001, p. 3. Available online at *http://www.heritage.org/Research/NationalSecurity/loader.cfm?url=/commonspot/security/getfile.cfm&PageID=7282.*

12 Ibid.

Counterpoint: Antiterror Laws Are Ineffective and Dangerous

1 Whitbeck, p. 52.

2 Center for Constitutional Rights, *The State of Civil Liberties,* p. 10. Available online at *http://www.ccr-ny.org/v2/reports/docs/Civil_Liberties.pdf.*

3 Eric Lichtblau, "U.S. Uses Terror Law to Pursue Crimes From Drugs to Swindling," *The New York Times,* September 28, 2003.

4 Ibid.

5 American Civil Liberties Union, Section 215 FAQ. New York: American Civil Liberties Union, 2002. Available online at *http://www.aclu.org/Privacy/Privacy.cfm?ID=11054&c=130.*

6 *Center for National Security Studies* v. *Department of Justice,* 331 F.3d 918, 947 (D.C. Cir. 2003) (Tatel, J., dissenting).

7 Ronald Dworkin, "Terror & the Attack on Civil Liberties," *New York Review of Books* 50, November 6, 2003, p. 17. Available online at *http://www.nybooks.com/articles/16738.*

8 U.S. Department of Transportation. Traffic Safety Facts, 2001. Available online at *http://www.dot.gov.*

9 David Aaron, "The New Twilight Struggle: Old Echoes of Vietnam in a New War Against Terror," *The American Prospect* 12, October 22, 2001, p. 18. Available online at *http://www.prospect.org/print/V12/18/aaron-d.html.*

10 Senator Russell Feingold, "On Opposing the U.S.A. Patriot Act." Address to the Associated Press Managing Editors Conference, Milwaukee, Wisconsin, October 12, 2001. Available online at *http://www.archipelago.org/vol6-2/feingold.htm.*

11 Ibid.

12 Gregg Krupa and John Bebow, "Immigration Crackdown Snares Arabs," *The Detroit News*, November 3, 2003.

13 Gore, "Freedom and Security." Available online at *http://www.moveon.org/gore/speech2.html*.

Conclusion

1 Office of the President, *National Security Strategy*, p. 31. Available online at *http://www.whitehouse.gov/nsc/nss.pdf*.

2 Senate Bill 1709, 108th Congress.

3 Richard Durbin, "Bipartisan Group of Senators Unveil 'Safe Act,'" October 15, 2003. Available online at *http://durbin.senate.gov/~durbin/new2001/press/2003/10/2003A17725.html*.

4 §374, Public Law 108-177, the Intelligence Authorization Act for Fiscal Year 2004.

5 George W. Bush, State of the Union Address, January 20, 2004. Available online at *http://www.whitehouse.gov/news/releases/2004/01/print/20040120-7.html*.

6 Bob Barr, "Patriot Act Games: It Can Happen Here," *The American Spectator* 36, August/September 2003, p. 34. Available online at *http://www.bobbarr.org/default.asp?pt=newsdescr&RI=440*.

7 Samuel P. Huntington, "The Clash of Civilizations," 72 Foreign Aff. 22 (1993).

8 Editorial, "W Ducks Real Nature of War U.S. is In," *New York Daily News*, October 29, 2003.

9 Walter Laqueur, "Postmodern Terrorism," In Charles W. Kegley, Jr., ed., *The New Global Terrorism: Characteristics, Causes, Controls*. Upper Saddle River, NJ: Prentice-Hall, 2003, p. 158.

10 David Rohde, "Radical Islam Gains a Seductive New Voice," *The New York Times*, October 26, 2003.

11 George W. Bush, Address to Joint Session of Congress, September 20, 2001. Available online at *http://www.whitehouse.gov/news/releases/2001/09/print/20010920-8.html*.

12 Dworkin, p. 17.

13 Benjamin and Simon, p. 411.

14 Ibid., p. 419.

Books

Benjamin, Daniel, and Steven Simon. *The Age of Sacred Terror.* New York: Random House, 2002.

Boot, Max. *The Savage Wars of Peace: Small Wars and the Rise of American Power.* New York: Basic Books, 2002.

Henderson, Harry. *Global Terrorism: The Complete Reference Guide.* New York: Checkmark Books, 2001.

Kegley, Charles W., Jr., ed. *The New Global Terrorism: Characteristics, Causes, Controls.* Upper Saddle River, NJ: Prentice-Hall, 2003.

Rehnquist, William H. *All Laws But One: Civil Liberties in Wartime.* New York: Alfred A. Knopf, 1998.

Websites

American Civil Liberties Union
http://www.aclu.org
The nation's oldest and best-known civil-liberties organization.

American Library Association
http://www.ala.org
The oldest and largest library association in the world monitors the library-related implementation of the USA Patriot Act.

Association of the Bar of the City of New York
http://www.abcny.org/pdf/should_the_laws.pdf
Online publication of the report, "Inter Arma Silent Leges? *In Time of Armed Conflict,* Should *the Laws Be Silent?*" 2001.

Brookings Institute
http://www.brookings.org
Some of this organization's scholars have been critical of the Bush Doctrine.

Center for Constitutional Rights
http://www.ccr-ny.org
A non-profit legal and educational organization dedicated to protecting and advancing the rights guaranteed by the U.S. Constitution and the Universal Declaration of Human Rights. This group is critical of the war in Iraq.

Council on Foreign Relations
http://www.terrorismanswers.com
A nonpartisan membership organization, research center, and publisher, the CFR is dedicated to increasing America's understanding of the world and contributing ideas to U.S. foreign policy.

Department of State

http://www.state.gov

Part of the Bush administration, this department is responsible for foreign policy.

Electronic Privacy Information Center

http://www.epic.org

This pro-privacy organization opposes the Patriot Act.

Hoover Institution, Stanford University

http://www-hoover.stanford.edu

This think tank is devoted to research in domestic policy and international affairs.

Life and Liberty (Justice Department)

http://www.lifeandliberty.gov

Provides arguments in favor of the Patriot Act.

Office of the President of the United States

http://www.whitehouse.gov/nsc/nss.pdf

Online publication of the report, *The National Security Strategy of the United States of America.* 2002.

Project for the New American Century

http://www.newamericancentury.org

Neoconservative think tank that supports the Bush Doctrine.

The White House

http://www.whitehouse.gov

Contains an archive of the president's speeches.

U.S. Army War College

http://www.carlisle.army.mil/ssi/pubs/2003/bounding/bounding.pdf

Online publication of report by Jeffrey Record, *Bounding the Global War on Terrorism.* 2003.

Cases and Statutes

Ex Parte Milligan.

A Civil War-era decision holding that a military commission could not try a civilian when the criminal courts were open, and the civilian's home state was neither in rebellion against the government nor threatened with invasion.

Ex Parte Quirin.

Held that German agents sent by the Nazis to commit sabotage inside the United States could be tried by a military commission because they were fighting while out of uniform and therefore violated the law of armed conflict.

Hamdi v. *Rumsfeld.*

Held that an American citizen, captured overseas while allegedly fighting against U.S. forces, had the right to challenge the government's decision to declare him an "enemy combatant" and detain him indefinitely.

Hirabayashi v. *United States.*

The first of the "Japanese exclusion cases" challenging the forced relocation of Japanese Americans to internment camps. It upheld the conviction of a Japanese American for violating a curfew in a military area.

In re Sealed Case.

Upheld the Patriot Act's new standard for conducting "foreign intelligence" surveillance—namely, that surveillance is permissible if obtaining foreign-intelligence information is a "significant purpose" rather than "the purpose."

Korematsu v. *United States.*

The second Japanese exclusion case. It upheld the conviction of a Japanese American for violating an order excluding members of his race from military areas. The case did not rule on whether the internment of Japanese Americans was constitutional.

Public Act 107-40. Authorization for the Use of Military Force.

A congressional resolution, passed in the wake of the September 11 attacks, authorizing the President to use military force against those responsible.

Public Act 107-56. The USA Patriot Act.

A comprehensive revision of federal laws, especially the criminal code, aimed at giving the government broader powers to investigate and punish terrorism and other serious crime.

Rasul v. *Bush.*

Held that non-U.S. citizens, captured overseas by American forces and held as enemy combatants at the Guantanamo Naval Base, had the legal right to challenge their indefinite detention.

Rumsfeld v. *Padilla (appeals court decision).*

Held that the President's Commander-in-Chief power was not broad enough to justify detaining an American, seized inside the United States and away from a combat zone, as an enemy combatant.

Terms and Concepts

al Qaeda

Bush Doctrine

civil liberties

"clash of civilizations"

commander-in-chief

criminal procedure

due process of law

enemy combatant

Guantanamo

habeas corpus

human rights

international law

Islam

law of armed conflict

military commission

national security

Osama bin Laden

Patriot Act

pre-emptive war

prisoners of war

profiling

Saddam Hussein

September 11

surveillance

Taliban

terrorism

unilateralism

United Nations

War Powers Resolution

weapons of mass destruction

Beginning Legal Research

The goal of POINT/COUNTERPOINT is not only to provide the reader with an introduction to a controversial issue affecting society, but also to encourage the reader to explore the issue more fully. This appendix, then, is meant to serve as a guide to the reader in researching the current state of the law as well as exploring some of the public-policy arguments as to why existing laws should be changed or new laws are needed.

Like many types of research, legal research has become much faster and more accessible with the invention of the Internet. This appendix discusses some of the best starting points, but of course "surfing the Net" will uncover endless additional sources of information—some more reliable than others. Some important sources of law are not yet available on the Internet, but these can generally be found at the larger public and university libraries. Librarians usually are happy to point patrons in the right direction.

The most important source of law in the United States is the Constitution. Originally enacted in 1787, the Constitution outlines the structure of our federal government and sets limits on the types of laws that the federal government and state governments can pass. Through the centuries, a number of amendments have been added to or changed in the Constitution, most notably the first ten amendments, known collectively as the Bill of Rights, which guarantee important civil liberties. Each state also has its own constitution, many of which are similar to the U.S. Constitution. It is important to be familiar with the U.S. Constitution because so many of our laws are affected by its requirements. State constitutions often provide protections of individual rights that are even stronger than those set forth in the U.S. Constitution.

Within the guidelines of the U.S. Constitution, Congress—both the House of Representatives and the Senate—passes bills that are either vetoed or signed into law by the President. After the passage of the law, it becomes part of the United States Code, which is the official compilation of federal laws. The state legislatures use a similar process, in which bills become law when signed by the state's governor. Each state has its own official set of laws, some of which are published by the state and some of which are published by commercial publishers. The U.S. Code and the state codes are an important source of legal research; generally, legislators make efforts to make the language of the law as clear as possible.

However, reading the text of a federal or state law generally provides only part of the picture. In the American system of government, after the legislature passes laws and the executive (U.S. President or state governor) signs them, it is up to the judicial branch of the government, the court system, to interpret the laws and decide whether they violate any provision of the Constitution. At the state level, each state's supreme court has the ultimate authority in determining what a law means and whether or not it violates the state constitution. However, the federal courts—headed by the U.S. Supreme Court—can review state laws and court decisions to determine whether they violate federal laws or the U.S. Constitution. For example, a state court may find that a particular criminal law is valid under the state's constitution, but a federal court may then review the state court's decision and determine that the law is invalid under the U.S. Constitution.

It is important, then, to read court decisions when doing legal research. The Constitution uses language that is intentionally very general—for example, prohibiting "unreasonable searches and seizures" by the police—and court cases often provide more guidance. For example, the U.S. Supreme Court's 2001 decision in *Kyllo* v. *United States* held that scanning the outside of a person's house using a heat sensor to determine whether the person is growing marijuana is unreasonable—*if* it is done without a search warrant secured from a judge. Supreme Court decisions provide the most definitive explanation of the law of the land, and it is therefore important to include these in research. Often, when the Supreme Court has not decided a case on a particular issue, a decision by a federal appeals court or a state supreme court can provide guidance; but just as laws and constitutions can vary from state to state, so can federal courts be split on a particular interpretation of federal law or the U.S. Constitution. For example, federal appeals courts in Louisiana and California may reach opposite conclusions in similar cases.

Lawyers and courts refer to statutes and court decisions through a formal system of citations. Use of these citations reveals which court made the decision (or which legislature passed the statute) and when and enables the reader to locate the statute or court case quickly in a law library. For example, the legendary Supreme Court case *Brown* v. *Board of Education* has the legal citation 347 U.S. 483 (1954). At a law library, this 1954 decision can be found on page 483 of volume 347 of the U.S. Reports, the official collection of the Supreme Court's decisions. Citations can also be helpful in locating court cases on the Internet.

Understanding the current state of the law leads only to a partial under-standing of the issues covered by the POINT/COUNTERPOINT series. For a fuller understanding of the issues, it is necessary to look at public-policy arguments that the current state of the law is not adequately addressing the issue. Many groups lobby for new legislation or changes to existing legislation; the National Rifle Association (NRA), for example, lobbies Congress and the state legislatures constantly to make existing gun control laws less restrictive and not to pass additional laws. The NRA and other groups dedicated to various causes might also intervene in pending court cases: a group such as Planned Parenthood might file a brief *amicus curiae* (as "a friend of the court")—called an "amicus brief"—in a lawsuit that could affect abortion rights. Interest groups also use the media to influence public opinion, issuing press releases and frequently appearing in interviews on news programs and talk shows. The books in POINT/COUNTERPOINT list some of the interest groups that are active in the issue at hand, but in each case there are countless other groups working at the local, state, and national levels. It is important to read everything with a critical eye, for sometimes interest groups present information in a way that can be read only to their advantage. The informed reader must always look for bias.

Finding sources of legal information on the Internet is relatively simple thanks to "portal" sites such as FindLaw (*www.findlaw.com*), which provides access to a variety of constitutions, statutes, court opinions, law review articles, news articles, and other resources—including all Supreme Court decisions issued since 1893. Other useful sources of information include the U.S. Government Printing Office (*www.gpo.gov*), which contains a complete copy of the U.S. Code, and the Library of Congress's THOMAS system (*thomas.loc.gov*), which offers access to bills pending before Congress as well as recently passed laws. Of course, the Internet changes every second of every day, so it is best to do some independent searching. Most cases, studies, and opinions that are cited or referred to in public debate can be found online— and *everything* can be found in one library or another.

The Internet can provide a basic understanding of most important legal issues, but not all sources can be found there. To find some documents it is necessary to visit the law library of a university or a public law library; some cities have public law libraries, and many library systems keep legal documents at the main branch. On the following page are some common citation forms.

COMMON CITATION FORMS

Source of Law	Sample Citation	Notes
U.S. Supreme Court	*Employment Division v. Smith,* 485 U.S. 660 (1988)	The U.S. Reports is the official record of Supreme Court decisions. There is also an unofficial Supreme Court ("S. Ct.") reporter.
U.S. Court of Appeals	*United States* v. *Lambert,* 695 F.2d 536 (11th Cir. 1983)	Appellate cases appear in the Federal Reporter, designated by "F." The 11th Circuit has jurisdiction in Alabama, Florida, and Georgia.
U.S. District Court	*Carillon Importers, Ltd.* v. *Frank Pesce Group, Inc.,* 913 F.Supp. 1559 (S.D.Fla. 1996)	Federal trial-level decisions are reported in the Federal Supplement ("F. Supp."). Some states have multiple federal districts; this case originated in the Southern District of Florida.
U.S. Code	Thomas Jefferson Commemoration Commission Act, 36 U.S.C., §149 (2002)	Sometimes the popular names of legislation—names with which the public may be familiar—are included with the U.S. Code citation.
State Supreme Court	*Sterling* v. *Cupp,* 290 Ore. 611, 614, 625 P.2d 123, 126 (1981)	The Oregon Supreme Court decision is reported in both the state's reporter and the Pacific regional reporter.
State Statute	Pennsylvania Abortion Control Act of 1982, 18 Pa. Cons. Stat. 3203-3220 (1990)	States use many different citation formats for their statutes.

INDEX

page:
76: Associated Press Graphics
84: Associated Press Graphics
92: Associated Press Graphics

Cover: Associated Press, AP/LISA POOLE

PAUL RUSCHMANN, J.D., is a legal analyst and writer based in Canton, Michigan. He received his undergraduate degree from the University of Notre Dame and his law degree from the University of Michigan. He is a member of the State Bar of Michigan. His areas of specialization include legislation, public safety, traffic and transportation, and trade regulation. He is also the author of *Legalizing Marijuana* and *Mandatory Military Service*, other titles in the POINT/COUNTERPOINT series. He can be found on line at *www.PaulRuschmann.com*.

ALAN MARZILLI, M.A., J.D., of Durham, North Carolina, is an independent consultant working on several ongoing projects for state and federal government agencies and nonprofit organizations. He has spoken about mental health issues in thirty states, the District of Columbia, and Puerto Rico; his work includes training mental health administrators, nonprofit management and staff, and people with mental illness and their family members on a wide variety of topics, including effective advocacy, community-based mental health services, and housing. He has written several handbooks and training curricula that are used nationally. He managed statewide and national mental health advocacy programs and worked for several public interest lobbying organizations in Washington, D.C., while studying law at Georgetown University.

363.32 War 2005
Ruschmann, Paul.
The war on terror
    30519007164810